TIJUANA

TIJUANA

Stories on the Border

Federico Campbell

Translated and introduced by
Debra A. Castillo

UNIVERSITY OF CALIFORNIA PRESS
BERKELEY LOS ANGELES LONDON

Originally published as *Tijuanenses*
© 1989 Editorial Joaquín Mortiz, Mexico City

The publisher gratefully acknowledges the Hull Memorial Fund at
Cornell University for financial support of this translation.

The author gratefully acknowledges Guillermo Sheridan, who first edited and
published *Tijuaneses* in *Revista de la Universidad de Mexico*.

University of California Press
Berkeley and Los Angeles, California

University of California Press, Ltd.
London, England

Library of Congress Cataloging-in-Publication Data

Campbell, Federico.
    [Tijuanenses. English]
    Tijuana: stories on the border / Federico Campbell; translated
and introduced by Debra A. Castillo.
        p.   cm.
    Includes bibliographical references.
    ISBN 0-520-08946-4 (alk. paper).—ISBN 0-520-08603-1 (alk. paper
: pbk.)
    1. Tijuana (Baja California, Mexico)—Fiction. I. Castillo,
Debra A. II. Title.
PQ7298.13.A392T5413   1995
863—dc20   94-9498
                                                                 CIP

Printed in the United States of America
9 8 7 6 5 4 3 2 1

The paper used in this publication meets the minimum requirements of
American National Standard for Information Sciences—Permanence of
Paper for Printed Library Materials, ANSI Z39.48-1984.

To Federico, my son

Contents

Borderlining: An Introduction

I played hopscotch at the border
men in green smile their green smiles
never ask me for papers, my skin is light
I crossed the border at least two hundred times
border linea abstract barrier
between my two concrete worlds.

Gina Valdes[1]

The border looked thin, except at crossing.

Jorge Guitart[2]

In an article on the cultural impact of the North American Free Trade Agreement, Carlos Monsiváis suggests that the old definition of Mexican identity—most famously articulated by Octavio Paz in his controversial 1950s best-seller, *Labyrinth of Solitude*—is based on a binary play of opposites: civilization vs. barbarism, Mexico City vs. the provinces, culture vs. desolation. This simplistic "us and them" conception of national identity is breaking down in the face of the northern border's ever-more insistent presence as an important cultural and commercial resource.

The borderlands contain several of Mexico's largest and richest cities, Monterrey and Tijuana among them. Their economic and cultural growth has disrupted traditional migration patterns from the country to the city so that Mexico City is no longer the sole force attracting provincial citizens trying to make good. In fact, it is the

border's simultaneous liminality and centrality that chal-
lenges Paz's and other's ways of thinking about Mexican
identity. Monsiváis is right in pointing out that Paz's con-
clusions, and those of his followers, are based on a form
of social organization that is no longer valid. The im-
pingement of the border on national awareness, then, requires moving away from a national self-concept imagined in such outdated terms. Indeed, as the January 1994
uprising in the southern border state of Chiapas confirmed, the provinces have mobilized themselves without
the mediation by Mexico City that central Mexican pun-
dits would once have assumed to be a necessary precon-
dition for any well-founded social or political movement.
The provinces are getting their demands for attention and
basic rights met, are exerting influence on national politics, and are forcing a reexamination of national identity.

Likewise, the citizens of the provinces have become
mobile along alternate routes, choosing, for instance, to
move to a border city rather than to Mexico City in search
of better economic and social opportunities. Such movement has in effect provoked a continual transformation
in the national consciousness, a transformation that
takes place along with a circulation of goods, people, and
culture among various rural settings and urban centers.

The cultural shock taking place at the border between
U.S.- and Mexico-based concepts of themselves and each
other redefines on a daily basis the limitations of identities constructed both regionally and nationally. Monsiváis points to "the certified absence of regional traditions
and the fact that the 'typical northerner' derives directly
from the culture industry, from the opportunistic and
commercial use of nationalism, the sincere and sentimental use of nationalism. On the northern border, Mexicanness is, at one and the same time, a heartfelt choice,

a defensive shield, and a sporadic mask . . ."³ When "Mexicanness" becomes both a matter of choice and a product of popular culture, then we know that we have left Mexico City and the agonizing soul-searching of Octavio Paz far behind, and are entering Tijuana and the world of Federico Campbell.

I. TIJUANA

There are at least half-a-dozen versions of the story behind the origin of Tijuana's name, all advanced more or less seriously and all of which ring true to some facet of the city's image. One version says that *Ti-wan* (city by the sea) was corrupted into "Ranchería de Ti Juan" or "Tía Juana" by Governor José María de Echendía when he established his presence in the area during the 1820s. Others trace the name to *Ticuan* or *Tecuam* (turtle), which, depending on the version of the story, derives from either the clan affiliation of the Cochimi chiefs or the former name of the mountain now known as Cerro Colorado. *Teguana* (inhospitable place or place without food) supposedly captures the Cochimi's frustration with the area's poor agricultural quality. Alternatively, some sources derive the city's name from references to an abundance of food: "Tía Juana," in this popular version of the town's origin, was the affectionate name for an extremely hospitable woman from Sonora who established herself in the area; she became so well known as a wonderful cook that people came from far and wide to sample her cuisine, and a small town sprang up around her to handle all the hungry visitors.

Tijuana has been relocated several times—partly because of disastrous floods—and has gone through numerous boom-and-bust cycles. At the end of the Mexican-

American War the 1848 Treaty of Guadalupe Hidalgo separated the small town from the Port of San Diego; the arrival of the Tijuana & Tecate Railroad in 1907 consolidated Tijuana's ties to its nearest neighbor, the United States, rather than to the Mexican center of power in the more distant Mexico City. More than one kind of tourist arrived on the train from the north; in 1911 Mexican president Porfirio Díaz wrote to U.S. president William Taft to complain about excursion trains crossing the border in the middle of the Mexican Revolution: "Every time we have a battle your people run excursion trains to the border. This causes embarrassment and interferes with the discipline of our troops as your girls make cat-calls to my men. Your people are buying the loot of Tijuana from Madero's rebels. . . . There are many other things we could complain of but if these rules are observed we can fight out this war in peace."[4]

Tijuana remained very small until Prohibition brought U.S. developers to the city. They built the luxurious Agua Caliente casino, where the West Coast's beautiful people came to dance under a gold-leaf ceiling and to gamble with $50 gold pieces. Rita Hayworth and her father, billed as the "Casinos," danced the flamenco there; Charlie Chaplin and Buster Keaton were regulars. Where the celebrities came to play there followed many other less newsworthy tourists who filled the many less-exclusive casinos, bars, and brothels, took excursions to the hot springs, and bet on the horse races. The consequences were sometimes curious and unexpected. So many people flocked to Tijuana on July 4, 1920 that San Diego ran out of gas and had to ration fuel.[5] The repeal of Prohibition began the town's slow slide into an emphasis on less luxurious forms of vice. In 1937 Mexican President Lázaro Cárdenas nationalized the casino and, perhaps with the intent of reorienting Tijuana's unfortunate international image, ordered it converted into a school.[6]

Today Tijuana still has not superseded its reputation as an international flea market and sin city. That image accounts for a large percentage of its extremely high volume of tourism from the United States (with between forty and fifty million *legal* crossings a year, Tijuana is the busiest point on the border, perhaps the busiest border in the world). The volatile combination of brothels and velvet paintings of Elvis Presley or Emiliano Zapata seems to underlie the put-down "It's *so* TJ," which is frequently heard among Californian Mexican-Americans. For many people TJ embodies a flagrant and tasteless "rascuachismo."[7] Others suspect that the garishness is all part of the act, a way of playing to expectations from the other side. As Grahame Greene wrote in 1983, "The border means more than a customs house, a passport officer, a man with a gun. Over there everything is going to be different."[8] I think of Greene's words as I hum the catchy tune of a song by the border-born singer and international musical phenomenon, Juan Gabriel: "Todo es diferente; todo, todo es diferente: la frontera." Greene's and Gabriel's definitions of difference respond to totally divergent sets of expectations about what Mexicans are like, what gringos are like, and what the border represents to both groups. And yet both Greene and Gabriel highlight "difference" as the border's primary feature.

One difference in the two groups' border experiences relates to the borderlands' imbrication in U.S. affairs. This close tie gives inhabitants from both sides a commonality they do not share with the people from the interiors of their respective countries. The influence of the United States is felt intensely throughout Mexico, not

only in relation to its economic and political power and
its technological expertise, but also by way of its television programming, its movie and rock stars, and its fast-
food chains. This influence sparks a continual process of
cultural exchange, though it is frequently underrecog-
nized, that occurs in all parts of the country but takes on
particular significance at the border. Interviews with Tijuana teenagers show that unlike their rock-fan counter-
parts in central Mexico who have to imagine what the
U.S. scene looks like, mainly on the basis of television and
movies, for the Tijuanans visiting the United States someday is not a distant dream: 41 percent go across the border during any given week, and only 11 percent have
never gone across at all. Thus they speak with the same
ease about San Diego's planetarium and shopping malls
as they do about similar places in their hometown. They
watch U.S. television programs, and, in a survey con-
ducted by Néstor García Canclini, they indicate that they
prefer U.S. radio stations to Mexican ones and that their
musical preferences tend toward rock rather than Mexican folklore.[9] At the same time, as García Canclini per-
ceptively notes, "Given their experience at the margin of
U.S. culture, [Baja Californians] are not as susceptible to
its glamour as Mexicans of the more distant capital."[10]
The impact of the U.S., then, is both greater and more
judiciously mediated in the borderlands. If greater familiarity in some cases breeds contempt, then it also offers
a way of personally experiencing the language, food, architecture, popular culture, and social interactions common to people from "the other side."

Two Tijuana anecdotes capture the instability and the
state of flux between two cultures that are seen as options
to be picked up and discarded at will:

"You don't use a passport?"

"No, because I was born on the other side, but I have a birth certificate in Tijuana. So when they ask me where I was born, I have to say 'here.' Or there, depending on whom I am answering."[11]

A photograph that we took by chance while walking down the Agua Caliente Boulevard provided us with a sudden synthesis: next to a poster that recommends "rock en tu idioma," was one written in English for a Mexican beverage [Don Pancho Coffe Liqueur (*sic*)]. When we are talking about language, ¿cuál es the other choice?[12]

This fluidity of identity that requires no passport to establish home ground in one place or another is echoed on another level with the unexpected juxtaposition of two Tijuana street signs and the real undecidability between the two major languages of public exchange and commerce. In such a context critics note, "even for the most monolingual of Latinos, the 'other' language looms constantly as a potential resource, and the option to vary according to different speech contexts is used far more often than not."[13]

If familiarity with the United States has mitigated the glamour of the other side, the Tijuanan businesspeople are still well aware that a large part of their city's revenue derives from maintaining a glamour of their own, an image of "difference" that will draw the tourists. So a bit of Spanish is mixed in with a bit of slightly distorted English, making the adventure both homey and defamiliarized at the same time, or the "rascuache" elements are played up, all in an effort to meet tourists' expectations. Unlike the southern parts of Mexico, say García Canclini's survey respondents, where the local people can count on the pyramids to pull in the tourist dollars, Tijuana never had much of anything to work with. Thus, says one

Tijuanan, "It's like we have to invent something for the gringos." And so, as Monsiváis and others have observed, they created a spurious difference. Today's Tijuana has more than one million inhabitants, over 60 percent of whom work in businesses directly or indirectly supported by tourism, and these are people cannily aware that U.S. citizens are not crossing the border to visit another good-sized modern city; they could go to Santa Barbara or Cincinnati for that experience. So Tijuana becomes TJ, projecting its difference. The dancing halls and brothels with their easily available alcohol and women feed one kind of fantasy. Other tourists buy big sombreros and get their pictures taken on stuffed burros painted with zebra stripes; as one Tijuanan commented in García Canclini's survey, "It responds to the myth that North Americans bring with them, that has to do with crossing the border into the past, into the primitive, into this thing about riding horses."[14] These tourists are in a sense crossing the border to enter into a Hollywood version of the U.S. frontier of a hundred years ago, with good guys and bad guys riding horses through shoot-'em-up cattle towns. Of course, since it is located in Mexico, TJ has to be both similar to those Hollywood dreams and slightly different, thus the silliness of sitting on a painted stuffed donkey rather than a horse.

In this transaction both sides are winners. The gringo tourists amuse themselves and confirm their superiority to themselves. Sitting on a zebra-ed donkey reminds them of the imaginary pleasures of riding a horse across the plains, but of course they are in Mexico, on a donkey, that stereotypical mount of the bumbling Mexican campesino rather than the regal and powerful steed of the all-American cowboy like the Lone Ranger. At the same time, the Tijuana businesspeople have a little harmless fun with the tourists who fall for the cheap made-for-tourists attractions.

The stereotype of the city as a place for cheap—and not always entirely safe—adventure is complicated by Tijuana's equally powerful reputation as a point of entry to the United States for illegal immigrants. The daytime flow heading south is, then, matched by a surreptitious nighttime flow heading north; the U.S. Border Patrol calls this section of the international border the "war zone." Every evening campfires dot the fields around the fence, helicopters take to the sky with searchlights, and Migra vans line up waiting for their first load. Caution signs on border highways showing a stereotypical image of an immigrant family in flight serve as a constant reminder to drivers in the area that people, and not just deer, flee across superhighways.

Such generalized perceptions leave the impression, however, that Tijuana is a city of transients of one kind or another: hopeful emigrants heading north, hopeful tourists heading south. It is important to remember that much of the city's recent growth derives from a generalized border boom in assembly plants (*maquiladoras*) and from its relative prosperity as an industrial center.[15] Tijuanans also have one of the highest rates of literacy in the country, with a high level of participation in cultural activities of all sorts on both sides of the border and a successful program of keeping young people in school through the junior-high level. This prosperity has triggered internal immigration from all parts of Mexico, thereby creating extremely rapid and unplanned growth with the attendant problems: lack of housing, water, sewage removal, health services, etc.

Concerned citizens and worried city planners see this crisis as both economic and moral, one which not only

stretches the city's resources but also activates the break-
down of the social fabric and produces behaviors ranging
from manifestations of psychological stress to criminal-
ity. This crisis is often framed imaginatively as a blocked
or bounded potentiality for development. As one inhabi-
tant put it, combining a frustrated utopianism with a concrete limitation, "It is the city of the future, but there is no
water."[16] Another Tijuanan poignantly pointed to the way
in which the borderline fence itself simultaneously serves
as a horizon that turns Tijuanans back upon themselves
and suggests the continuation of Tijuana on the other side,
in another space both temporal and spiritual: "I've always
thought that if there are monuments in Tijuana, there
ought to be a monument with that design. The fence is full
of symbolism. Those who emigrate always say, 'I crossed
the fence.' It represents a massive crossover, or an attempt
to cross, not just a political or geographical division."[17] The
possibility of border crossing in either direction, whether
acted upon or not, licenses dreams and permits the promiscuous cohabitation of different orders of reality. "Crossing," then, at the Tijuana/San Diego border is both a
metaphor for a spiritual passage and a specific space of
struggle and transgression.

II. TIJUANA: STORIES ON THE BORDER

Campbell's collection of short stories is part of a body of
literature only recently beginning to receive, in both Mexico and the United States, the recognition it deserves.
There is, in all of these eccentric texts, a different geo-
social awareness from that of mainstream works from
either country, a different linguistic texture, and a different relation to narrative agency. Like Rosina Conde and
Guadalupe Rivemar, Campbell describes the often gritty

and strident aspects of Tijuana's infamous nightclub scene; like Bárbara Jacobs, whose references range from the Spanish Civil War to San Francisco's hippie communities to the wars in Central America, Campbell too moves with ease and confidence between the depiction of a provincial childhood to convincing portrayals of the U.S. and Mexican metropolises of his adulthood.[18] Likewise, Campbell's work will be compared to Miguel Méndez's now-classic Chicano novel, *Pilgrims of Aztlán*.[19] In Méndez's novel, first published in Spanish in 1974, Tijuana serves as a metaphor of all that is wrong with the border culture created by the oppression of the United States. In style it is brisk and colloquial, using dialogue and staged vignettes to make its political point. In comparison to Méndez, Campbell's Tijuana is both more complex and less programmatically ideological. Campbell, unlike Méndez, describes a city that is struggling to define itself against the double pressures of the two great metropolitan centers that serve as its cultural and political reference points: D.F. (Mexico City) and L.A.

Campbell's stories graphically illustrate the confluence of many types of borders. One border is, of course, the political border between the United States and Mexico, physically impressed upon the consciousness of border dwellers in the form of the fence that slices through the San Diego–Tijuana metropolitan area. The fence, then, serves as a primary location and symbol. Some roads, suggest the narrators of this collection, lead up to the fence and then abruptly cease to exist. A few others break off at a border post presided over by an immigration officer, only to resume mysteriously, discontinuously, on the other side. Anyone who drives in the border region is always aware of the possibilities opened by the paved surface, and of the possibilities foreclosed. For people of the

two Californias the fence imposes itself as the most potent monument to their shared and divided history.

A second border is that between fiction and nonfiction.
Campbell draws freely on autobiographical elements and
crucial historical moments in Tijuana's history in con-
structing this volume. He was born in Tijuana in 1941,
the son of a telegraph-operator father and a school-
teacher mother, and he characterizes the Campbell side
of his family, like the characters in these stories, as ob-
servers of life rather than participants.[20] As is also true of
the characters here, Campbell has particularly potent
memories of trains and airplanes, and like the narrator
of *Everything About Seals*, he recalls with affection his
childhood vacations to Navojoa, of which he says: "A
sense of belonging follows my footsteps. I know myself
to be more complete here than in any other part of the
world. I do not have the slightest doubt that my name is
what it is. There is nothing left between the lines."[21]
Campbell's father's sudden death and his mother's long
and agonizing death from cancer also mark his life and
his style. Campbell says of his mother: "I listened to my
mother's voice all throughout those eighteen nights that
I spent at her side as she lay dying, not because the timbre
sounded like hers, but rather because there are internal
voices that one saves up: the voices that taught us to
speak, to learn a certain language, to name things, voices
that remain engraved forever giving us the first sense of
the world, a composition of place."[22] Both the sense of
place and the physicality of voice are very much present
in these stories.

In a similar way, Campbell calls up a number of crucial
elements in Tijuana's historical record: its early Incar-
nation as a mission settlement linked to other towns in
the area including Tecate, San Isidro, and San Diego; its

Prohibition boom, largely dependent upon the casino business; the closing of the casino and the depression following the end of Prohibition in the U.S.; the demographic explosion in the last few decades. These events all become part of the texture of the collection of stories, a constantly shifting backdrop to the narrators and their interlocutors.

A third border is created in the encounter between land and sea, and Campbell recurs frequently to the metaphor of that border as well. Land and sea answer to each other in this California coastal borderland, just as the U.S. and Mexico must: the two borders, seashore and fence, run perpendicular to each other. This perfect conversation, these competing and cacophonous monologues—of land and sea, United States and Mexico, fence and shoreline, English-speakers and Spanish-speakers—pervade both Californias. Humankind follows the surfaces of the land or the traceries of its roads; fish swim the sea roads, and only those strange, ambiguous creatures, the seals, easily slip back and forth across the borders between them. The seals, says the narrator of *Everything About Seals*, are "halfway beings; metamorphosed borderliners." The human border dwellers, Campbell suggests, are also "halfway beings" in some ways, perfectly at home in their own territories but ungainly, perhaps incomprehensible, or even mutilated, outside them.

Finally Campbell's stories ask us to reevaluate the ways in which we think of social interactions. Social theorist Roger Rouse has argued that multidirectional circuits of migration—for example, Mixtec-speaking Indians moving, on a regular schedule, from the Oaxacan highlands to California and then back to Oaxaca—force us to rethink conventional notions of social science in which migration from Mexico to the United States is presumed to

be unidirectional. Rouse explains how seasonal migration affects the small Mexican towns in the interior of the
country as well as the large cities on the border. Thus,
the Mixtec Indians may have only a rudimentary knowledge of Spanish and little or no contact with the central
Mexican government, yet they are bilingual in Mixtec and
English, have access to fax machines and VCRs, and have
developed sophisticated means of keeping the lines of
communication with the United States open.

The braceros who come north to work in the U.S. in-
teract with the United States and its cultural products,
and they bring some of these ideas and products back
with them to Mexico. The migrants who cross the border
and decide to stay in California, becoming part of an in-
creasingly internationalized Latino population in that
state, add their visions and perspectives to the ever-shift-
ing California identity. Rouse concludes that, in this
sense, the borderlands become only the most obvious
case of a general deterritorializing drive imperative op-
erative in many societies.[23] It is one that requires an alternative mental cartography, one based on the notion of
the border rather than on traditional, and largely superseded, concepts such as community or nation.[24] Campbell
would agree with this notion of an alternative mental
cartography, but he would also insist on remembering
the specificity of the Tijuanan perspective on this issue.
"We live in different, divided worlds," the narrator of *Everything About Seals* says to Beverly, the woman who ob-
sesses him; he is both right and wrong in his assertion,
since what divides the two characters is also the basis of
their common identity. Campbell's starkly poetic novella
ends abruptly, and the truncation of the novella, with its
narrator's fall into the recital of meaningless common-
place courtesies, reminds us of how *situated* discussions

of border reality, border identity, and border politics tend to be.

Campbell's poetic meditation on this complexly cross-cultural territory stimulates literary critics and cultural theorists to look beyond traditional disciplinary boundaries to find new ways of speaking and interacting. "What is unraveling now," says a recent article on the pachuco/pachuca, "is the discursive formation of a discipline—the conjunctural effects of its practices, institutions, technologies, and strategies of explanation."[25] This unraveling is particularly noticeable in borderline texts like Campbell's that focus on the lives and identities of border dwellers. Art from the borderlands, like Campbell's writing, cannot easily be accommodated to the cultural histories of either nation. Says Campbell in *Insurgentes Big Sur*, "And you'd turn your gaze from one side to another, from Los Angeles to the DF and vice versa, like in a Ping-Pong game. You couldn't decide very easily which of the two poles most attracted you, it wasn't ever very clear to you if the innovations in speech or dress . . . came from Tepito or from the East Side." In the Ping-Pong view, central Mexican culture and the Spanish language exert a strong pull from one side, but Los Angeles's popular culture and the appeal of a secure income exert an equal and opposite attraction: "Where have you been, in Los Angeles?" asks a character in *Tijuana Times,* and the narrator muses, "The question presupposes a myth. Every absence is related to an adult destiny on Los Angeles's East Side." The constant to-and-fro from LA to the DF also defines the narrator of *Everything About Seals,* a character who longs for safe limits— but not the limits imposed from outside, of a reality circumscribed by an all-too-real fence.

These stories not only mark, but also provoke a certain kind of internal cultural crisis in narrowly conceived ideas about the definitions of nation and nationalism. Furthermore, while these stories in no way endorse the kind of violent conflicts that often result from the friction between cultures in the border region, they do illustrate how assumptions about gender roles, personal politics, and appropriations of authority are played out in these regions of cultural miscegenation.

III. FEDERICO CAMPBELL

Federico Campbell, who was born in Tijuana in 1941, has written one other work of fiction, a novel loosely based on the 1968 student demonstrations in Mexico City and entitled *Pretexta (o el cronista enmascarado)* (Pretext [or the masked chronicler]). He is, however, best known in Mexico for his work as a reporter and a journalism teacher. After studying law and philosophy at the National Autonomous University of Mexico from 1960 to 1965, Campbell dedicated himself to what would become his primary career, journalism. His work has been published in Mexican newspapers such as *El Día*, *Excélsior*, and *Siempre!*, as well as in South American publications like *Marcha*, *Amaru*, and *El Nacional*. In 1967 he obtained a scholarship from the World Press Institute in Saint Paul, Minnesota, and for a period of time he worked with the *Hartford (Conn.) Courant*. In 1969 he became the Washington, D.C., correspondent for the Mexican news agency.

Between 1973 and 1977 Campbell edited the journal *Mundo médico* (Medical world), and he founded a small press, La Máquina de Escribir, in 1977. From 1977 to 1988 Campbell worked as a reporter for the weekly journal *Proceso*. In 1990 he was recognized with a major award from the Consejo Nacional para la Cultura y las

Artes (National Council for Arts and Culture), and since 1991 he has been a member of the Association of Investigative Reporters and Editors, which is headquartered at the University of Missouri. Campbell has also given free courses in journalism in several cities along the U.S./Mexico border.

His literary activities include translating plays, including works by William Shakespeare, Harold Pinter, David Mamet, and Leonardo Sciascia, from English and Italian into Spanish and authoring several volumes of essays and interviews as well as a journalism textbook. His works in progress include *La invención del poder* (The invention of power) and *Máscara negra* (Black mask), both of which are works of political philosophy, and a literary journal entitled *Post scriptum triste.*

IV. BORDER STUDIES AND AMERICAN STUDIES

It is not much of an exaggeration to say that in recent years the border in general, and Tijuana in particular, has become a magnet for theoretical work by philosophers, writers, and artists. French philosopher Michel de Certeau spent the last years of his life in San Diego, and his experiences there deeply influenced his contention that life is a constant crossing of borders.[26] *Borderlands/La frontera* by Texas social critic Gloria Anzaldúa is required reading in many university classrooms, and Tijuanan "border brujo" Guillermo Gómez Peña was awarded a MacArthur "genius" award for his sometimes scandalous performance art. On the other side of the border, Mexican writers and thinkers like Carlos Monsiváis, Néstor García Canclini, and Elena Poniatowska all point to the importance of considering Mexico's northern border in any serious reevaluation of Mexican culture and society. This recognition of the critical importance of border studies has been reaffirmed in more tangible ways as well: in 1982 the Colegio de la Frontera Norte (Northern Border College), which emphasizes research on border issues, opened in Tijuana.

Borderlands writers and thinkers argue for the need to grant equal status and validity to their point of view when ranged against American Studies' traditional privileging of a cross-Atlantic orientation; that is, American Studies tends to look to places like Great Britain and France for theoretical support rather than to Latin America or Asia. For example, Donna Haraway concludes that in theoretical debates too little attention has been paid to the politics of location, when in fact, geographical sites affect theoretical statements in critical ways. In an interchange with other scholars Haraway made this position clear: "It's a California statement I want to make. It has to do with seeing the world in relationship to Latin America. . . . living in conquest territory. . . . It's a sense of the Pacific."[27]

One of the attractions of the border area for scholars rests upon their perception that, unlike other geographical sites that have traditionally served as the location where abstract thinking originates, the border offers an alternative space featuring a flexible and mutating set of social and cultural arrangements. The border sets up a position for both living and thinking, one involving a sense of place as well as implicit displacement. It suggests a space that is both neatly divided and, in the crossover dreams of its inhabitants, disorientingly confused. Because of this feature, the border seems to many thinkers to be a particularly clear and forceful example of issues ranging from the political to the aesthetic, all of which are imagined less extremely, or articulated less clearly, in other situations. "It often occurred to me," writes García Canclini, "that, along with New York, Tijuana is one of the major laboratories of postmodernity."[28] Homi Bhabha goes even further when he hypothesizes that "where the transmission of 'national' traditions was once the major theme of a world literature, perhaps we can now suggest that transnational histories of migrants . . .—these border and frontier conditions—may be the terrains of World Literature."[29] Emily Hicks would agree that the border is both laboratory and canvas for many postmodern artists; yet, she reminds us, it is a version of postmodernity with a particular edginess: "What is most intriguing about border culture is its refusal of the emptiness of the U.S. post-modern culture of simulation, on the one hand, and its refusal of the rigidity of the folk and modernist cultures of Mexican nationalism and some Chicano nationalists, on the other."[30]

García Canclini (Mexico City), Hicks (San Diego), and Bhabha (Sussex, England) are all fascinated with the theoretical implications of borderlands studies, and all are working on parallel projects aimed at reconstructing and reinscribing the reciprocal exchanges that take place at the intersections of uneven and unequal abutting cultural structures. These theoretical discussions have another function beyond instilling an appreciation of the aesthetic implications. As Hicks suggests, and George Yúdice confirms, they return an awareness of ethical concerns to both narrative and theoretical acts.

The idea of a single *grand récit,* or generally understood master narrative, is itself a concept with political as well as aesthetic and theoretical implications. More importantly, the limitations of such abstract and universalizing

structures can be seen most clearly in the dissonant borderlands and peripheries of both societies and theoretical
structures. Yúdice writes:

> My argument as regards Latin America is not that informal econ-
> omies or narcotraffic *are* postmodern phenomena but, rather,
> that they are simultaneously responses and propositions that
> pose alternatives to the *grand récit* of postmodernity as it has
> been constructed by Lyotard, Jameson, and their predeces-
> sors. . . . How we (re)think modernity and postmodernity has
> consequences for how we construe the ethicopolitical goals of
> theory. Paz's poetics of reconciling opposites in the transhistory
> of the present leads to an antimodern irrationality with little
> room for accommodating the democratic demands of diverse
> social movements. Rethinking democracy outside the terms set
> by the *grand récit* of modernity is an enterprise many Latin
> American social movements see as necessary.[31]

What follows naturally from such a radical rethinking
of the *grand récits*, those of both modernity and postmodernity, is a rethinking, as well, of the nature of such concepts as nationalism and citizenship, which also need to
be revised to take into account the specificity and heter-
ogeneity of communities. When one moves into the borderlands, the crossing of cultures, languages, races, experiences, social statuses, and economic expectations
serve as an interrogation of such master narratives. Even
where mobility remains restricted, an awareness of the
potential for such crossings serves a similar function.
Thus, even for Tijuanans who never visit the United
States, an awareness of the existence of the fence continually reminds them of the potential for crossing, or not
crossing, to the other side. And, certainly, the fence and
the border guard, which enforce a legal definition of identity—documented or undocumented, also bring to the
forefront questions involving the differential treatment of
people based not only on citizenship, but also on factors

such as race and assumed social class. Likewise, along with critical practice sensitive to border issues is recognition that the idea of a single, absolute meaning (such as unequivocal answers to questions like "Who is Mexican?" and "What is Mexicanness?") is not so much lost as it is subject to negotiation, as are the other products of cultural conditioning. In such renegotiations of identity, cultural constructs are both eroded and reinforced. The querying of Mexicanness, as constructed alongside a northern border identity, is also a locus for recouping the memory of a slowly dying historical record from the general gravitation toward social amnesia, which has been noted by so many border scholars.

Border studies, accordingly, uncovers and provides a space for exploring the constructed nature of what Yúdice would call "ethics-talk" and "identity-talk." It also provides important examples of *how* such constructions are formulated and provides a starting point from which to begin to explore the pressures involved in both their evolution and their maintenance of these constructions.

And, to a certain extent, that is the lure of Tijuana for me, here in upstate New York.

NOTES

1. Gina Valdes, *Comiendo Lumbre: Eating Fire* (Pismo Beach, Calif.: Maize Press, 1986), 16.
2. Jorge Guitart, "On Borders," *Buffalo Arts Review* 3, no. 1 (1985): 5.
3. Carlos Monsiváis, "De la cultura mexicana en vísperas del Tratado de Libre Comercio," in *La educación y la cultura ante el Tratado de Libre Comercio,* eds. Gilberto Guevara Niebla and Néstor García Canclini (Mexico City: Nueva Imagen, 1992), 202.

4. June Nay Summers, *Buenos días, Tijuana* (Ramona, Calif.: Ballena Press, 1974), 26.

5. Ibid., 37.

6. Mexican anthropologist and culture critic Néstor García Canclini notes that the current residents of Tijuana have mixed feelings about Agua Caliente. They recall, for example, that the tower "was located elsewhere, burned down, and has been restored as the symbol of a past that in part tends to be denied. They say that its relocation in a different place corresponds to the reelaboration of a time now seen as displaced, denied, and relocated. They see in this removal a way of taking on their history: even though it is an exact replica, it is changed." Néstor García Canclini and Patricia Safa, *Tijuana: La casa de toda la gente* (Iztapalapa, Mexico: INAH-ENAH, Programa cultural de las fronteras, 1989), 53.

7. In a recent interview, Tomás Ybarra-Frausto defines "rascuachismo" as "an underclass sensibility that uses parodic expression and is rooted in particular forms of community culture." "Interview with Tomás Ibarra-Frausto," in *On Edge: The Crisis of Contemporary Latin American Culture,* eds. George Yúdice, Jean Franco, and Juan Flores (Minneapolis: University of Minnesota Press, 1992), 214.

8. Cited in Marcienne Rocard, "The Mexican-American Frontier: The Border in Mexican-American Folklore and Elite-lore," *Aztlan* 18 (1989):83.

9. García Canclini and Safa, *Tijuana,* 49–50.

10. Néstor García Canclini, "Cultural Reconversion," in *On Edge,* 42.

11. García Canclini and Safa, *Tijuana,* 47.

12. Ibid., 58.

13. Juan Flores and George Yúdice, "Living Borders/Buscando America: Languages of Latino Self-formation," *Social Text* 8, no. 2 (1990): 75.

14. García Canclini and Safa, *Tijuana,* 29.

15. The borderlands on the Mexican side are experiencing rapid growth because income in that area tends to be at least

three times higher than elsewhere in the country. I say this prosperity is "relative," however, since the Mexican border-dweller knows very well that the more prosperous "other side" still represents some of the most economically depressed regions of the United States. See Milton H. Jamail and Margo Gutiérrez, *The Border Guide* (Austin: University of Texas Press, 1992), 1–2.

16. García Canclini and Safa, *Tijuana*, 40.

17. Ibid., 45.

18. Rosina Conde is the author of numerous chapbooks and volumes of poetry. Among her narratives are *De infancia y adolescencia* (About childhood and adolescence) (Mexico City: Pantomima, 1982) and *En la tarima* (On the platform) (Mexico City: Universidad Autónoma Metropolitana, 1984). Guadalupe Rivemar's work, which has been published in various places, includes "El New Yorker," in *Memoria del primer encuentro de escritores de las Californias* (San Diego: SEBS-DAC, 1987) and "Regresamos" (We are going back) (*El Oficio* 5 [1987]). Bárbara Jacobs's best-known work is her autobiographical novel, *The Dead Leaves*, which focuses on her early life in Mexico with her Lebanese-American father and Mexican mother (trans. David Unger. Willimantic, Conn.: Curbstone, 1993).

19. Miguel Méndez, *Pilgrims of Aztlán*, trans. David William Foster (Tempe, Ariz: Bilingual Review/Press, 1993).

20. Federico Campbell, *De cuerpo entero* (Mexico City: Ediciones Corunda, 1990), 34.

21. Ibid., 16.

22. Ibid., 15.

23. The concept of "deterritorialization" comes from the influential works of French philosophers Gilles Deleuze and Félix Guattari: *Anti-Oedipus* (trans. Mark Hurley, Mark Seem, and Helen R. Lane [New York: Viking, 1977]) and *Kafka: Toward a Minor Literature* (trans. Dona Polan [Minneapolis: University of Minnesota Press, 1986]). They use the concept to describe how internationalization, polyglotism, political immediacy, and high technology all affect contemporary writing. The sense

of the term might be aptly captured for my purposes here by a familiar phrase often repeated by Chicano writers and artists: "From Aztec to high tech." I am indebted to D. Emily Hicks's *Border Writing: The Multidimensional Text* (Minneapolis: University of Minnesota Press, 1991) for her work in theorizing deterritorialization in the context of border culture.

24. Roger Rouse, "Mexicano, Chicano, Pocho: La migración mexicana y el espacio social del posmodernismo," *Unomásuno* (31 December 1988), *Página Uno* literary supplement: 1–2.

25. Marcos Sánchez-Tranquilino and John Tagg, "The Pachuco's Flayed Hide: Mobility, Identity, and *Buenas Garras,*" in *Cultural Studies,* eds. Lawrence Grossberg, Cary Nelson, and Paula Treichler (New York: Routledge, 1992), 557.

26. See Michel de Certeau, "Californie, un théatre de passants," *Autrement* 31 (April 1981): 10–18.

27. Donna Haraway, discussion period recording in *Cultural Studies,* 703.

28. García Canclini, "Cultural Reconversion," *On Edge,* 40.

29. Homi K. Bhabha, "The Home and the World," *Social Text* 10 (1992): 146.

30. D. Emily Hicks, "Review of Herbert Blau's The Eye of the Prey," unpublished manuscript, 1988, 32–33.

31. George Yúdice, "Postmodernism and Transnational Capitalism in Latin America," in *On Edge,* 4, 7.

SELECTED BIBLIOGRAPHY

Works by Federico Campbell

Conversaciones con escritores (interviews). Mexico City: Sep-Setentas, 1972.

De cuerpo entero (memoir). Mexico City: Ediciones Corunda, 1990.

Infame turba (interviews). Barcelona: Lumen, 1971.

La sombra de Serrano: De la matanza de Huitzilac a la explusión de Calles por Cárdenas (journalism collection). Mexico City: Proceso, 1980.

Memoria de Sciascia (essay). Mexico City: Fondo de Cultura
Económica, 1989.
Pretexta (o el cronista enmascarado) (novel). Mexico City:
Fondo de Cultura Económica, 1979.
Tijuanenses (stories). Mexico City: Joaquín Mortiz, 1989.

For Further Reading

Aguirre Bernal, Celso. *Tijuana: Su historia, sus hombres.* Mexicali: Imprenta Mexicali, 1975.

Anderson, Benedict. *Imagined Communities: Reflections on the Origin and Spread of Nationalism.* Rev. ed. New York: Verso, 1991.

Anzaldúa, Gloria. *Borderlands/La Frontera: The New Mestiza.* San Francisco: Spinsters/Aunt Lute Books, 1987.

Bhabha, Homi K. "The Home and the World." *Social Text* 10 (1992): 141–53.

———, ed. *Nation and Narration.* London: Routledge, 1990.

Flores, Juan, and George Yúdice. "Living Borders/Buscando America: Languages of Latino Self-formation." *Social Text* 8, no. 2 (1990): 57–84.

Franco, Jean. *Plotting Women: Gender and Representation in Mexico.* New York: Columbia University Press, 1989.

García Canclini, Néstor, and Patricia Safa. Photographs by Lourdes Grobet. *Tijuana: La casa de toda la gente.* Iztapalapa, Mexico: INAH-ENAH, Programa cultural de las fronteras, 1989.

García Nuñez, Fernando. "Notas sobre la frontera norte en la novela mexicana." *Cuadernos Americanos* 2, no. 10 (1988): 159–68.

Hicks, D. Emily. *Border Writing: The Multidimensional Text.* Minneapolis: University of Minnesota Press, 1991.

Jamail, Milton H., and Margo Gutiérrez. *The Border Guide.* Austin: University of Texas Press, 1992.

Monsiváis, Carlos. "De la cultura mexicana en vísperas del Tratado de Libre Comercio." In *La educación y la cultura ante el Tratado de Libre Comercio*, edited by Gilberto Guevara

Niebla and Néstor García Canclini. Mexico City: Nueva Imagen, 1992: pp. 190–209.

Paz, Octavio. *Labyrinth of Solitude.* Translated by Lysander Kemp. New York: Grove Press, 1961.

Remy, Anseleme. "The Unholy Trinity." *Caribbean Review* 6.2 (1974): 14–18.

Rocard, Marcienne. "The Mexican-American Frontier: The Border in Mexican-American Folklore and Elitelore." *Aztlan* 18 (1989): 83–94.

Rouse, Roger. "Mexicano, Chicano, Pocho: La migración mexicana y el espacio social del posmodernismo." *Unomásuno,* 31 December 1988, *Página Uno* literary supplement: 1–2.

Sánchez-Tranquilino, Marcos, and John Tagg. "The Pachuco's Flayed Hide: Mobility, Identity, and *Buenas Garras.*" In *Cultural Studies,* edited by Lawrence Grossberg, Cary Nelson, and Paula Treichler, 556–70. New York: Routledge, 1992.

Spillers, Hortense. "Who Cuts the Border? Some Readings on 'America.'" In *Comparative American Identities: Race, Sex, and Nationality in the Modern Text,* 1–25. New York: Routledge, 1991.

Summers, June Nay. *Buenos días, Tijuana.* Ramona, Calif.: Ballena Press, 1974.

Yúdice, George, Jean Franco, and Juan Flores, eds. *On Edge: The Crisis of Contemporary Latin American Culture.* Minneapolis: University of Minnesota Press, 1992.

Everything About Seals

And on the right hand of the Indies
there was an island called California,
to one side of earthly paradise, totally
populated by women without a single
man. They had strong, beautiful bodies
and were fiercely courageous and very
powerful. . . . Now and again men from
the mainland went there and lay with
them and if they bore female children,
they kept them, and if the babies were
boys, they threw them out of the
community.

Garci-Ordóñez de Montalvo
The Adventures of Esplandián, 1492

I

I can't really tell much difference between one city and another. I can land in places I've never seen before, and I drive around as if I had spent my whole life there. Wide streets and narrow streets, the architecture of the houses, none of it really catches my attention. Maybe only the movement of people and cars bewilders me and makes me wander from one place to another without heading anywhere in particular. It's all the same to me. Little by little the discrete qualities of things slip away, and almost every afternoon I end by falling asleep, then waking, and—naturally—not speaking to anybody. I have given myself truces: periods of time in which I postpone or occlude my desires. I am the center of the world, the mirror. Nothing matters and everything exists as an extension of my wishes. When I fall asleep things disappear, the earth stops spinning and ceases its progressive displacement through the universe.

The afternoons on the coast are chilly; they are as icy as the Pacific, as muted as the Alaskan current that descends along one side of the peninsula until it falls in a curve before the Sebastían Vizcaíno Bay. From the cotton fields along the flank of the desert plains one can make out the mountains to one side, the San Pedro Martir chain, and then, far off in the distance, the foamy white, dark blue sea. I lean back against an abandoned cart on the escarpment. The darkening sea seems pacified. I know that it is cold. Even by the lunar light, the sea cannot manage to draw the line that defines it against the background: a kind of black wind confuses the sea with the prolongation of the sky. I feel the breeze pick up and advance toward me. At some times of the year freighters parade past, sticking close to the shore, eluding the north wind, but soon they are lost to sight. Only once in a while, every two or three years, the same French ship passes by, leaving the ocean and heading toward the Panama Canal, and it signals the shore with a three-gun salute. A passenger on the foggy deck waves and makes offering signals with his bottle. The houses in the little villages are white, they are painted with lime, they climb the hills silently . . . The sea darkens and the sky also turns black and rain falls against the water; everything becomes obscure and chaotic. The wind makes me stupid and I scream for help. A herd of seals floats by, drifting with the Alaskan current. Further out, a fishing boat advances, only intermittently making its presence known with the on-and-off flashing of a signal light it must carry on its prow or stern.

"I'm cold."

By the time the sun has finally made an appearance, I have Beverly's belongings stored in the car.

"I'll drive," I tell her. "You sleep."

II

Although I believed at first that she had disappeared definitively, for several weeks the yearning to see her and the feeling that she would turn up on the day I least expected seemed to persist. As on other occasions when I suddenly found myself on the outskirts of the city, I once again began to visit the airport. The slope of the road itself made me slide into the curves of the hills; later, the gradual climb by bicycle allowed me to feel the change of temperature and the growing freshness of the air. As I came over the crest of the hill, the only point of reference for the ruins of Agua Caliente was the minaret of the casino down below, in an area set apart from the urban zone.

Going out to the airport was a very old habit; it was not a chance occurrence and it did not start with Beverly's presence there. Once upon a time, I made the same excursion by bicycle; I spent the morning hours climbing the hills and the rest of the day watching the airplanes on the flatlands where the airport was constructed. I never invited anyone to go with me. Nor did I ever share with anyone the happiness I found in this solitary pursuit. I liked to go alone. It was a fascinating spectacle that took me outside myself and made me forget the passage of time. During those first years, what arrived were small, double-winged planes. Later I learned about more recent models, like the DC-3 cargo planes that transported shell-fish, and I saw the first jet propulsion planes arrive, planes that took off in a blast of noise over the old, black tri-motor monoplane that, stripped of its propellers, rusted at the entrance to the hangars with a certain decrepit beauty, taking on the guise of a steel statue or a whale skeleton. In the skies above the international boundary line there also circled pairs of military hunters, distract-edly invading the airspaces of both countries, leaving vi-brating windows and painful eardrums in their wakes.

Watching planes take off and land fixated me on the ground to such a degree that my sight, and my whole body, entered into a kind of momentary paralysis, as if the buzzing of the machines absorbed me and trans-ported me from the spasmodic into silence. I watched them lose themselves, insert themselves into the sky be-hind a black stream, or set down on the landing strip like giant seagulls. The few times I actually traveled in an air-plane—once a few days before my father died, another time in the improvised backseat of a crop-dusting plane— I was filled with panic. I always tried to sleep during the flight, but that was impossible. By pretending I was asleep, I experienced a feeling of attraction, of being sus-pended in the air, of floating on or being sweetly im-mersed in a warm pool, well protected thanks to the four motors and the cockpit that carried me and rocked me and impeded my body's fall through the vacuum. With this false dream—because not even the purr of the motors lulled me to sleep—I rested my forehead against the win-dowpane and watched how my body and the body of the airplane sliced through clouds and slid along their white immensity. It struck me that running through a field scattered with cotton balls would not in any way save me from catastrophe. It occurred to me that I could die, and from that moment on I was unable to set down roots anywhere.

The fact of flying forced me to face a risk completely outside myself, and since I could do nothing to avoid it, the risk became attractive. It was a little bit like confronting the possibility of losing everything in the roulette game in the casino, and for that very reason wanting to weld myself authentically to something. I allowed these thoughts to flow through me while realizing at the same time that flying is a stationary mode. There is a suspension that feeds my laziness and allows me to play with forewarnings not unknown to me on solid land. I can bet blindly, I can wallow in the sensation that in my flight from real danger—danger that I have not dared to confront even experimentally in all of my thirty years of halfway life—I share the lives of men more audacious and less cowardly than I. The only thing I achieved was to meditate on my passive condition and my vital clumsiness, on my excessive caution and my misery. But, at any rate, this fantasized relaxation of flying and believing myself in confrontation with a ridiculous deathly danger didn't torment me all that much. The last time I flew, I saw the clouds, and later the clear spaces of the coast, the yellow mountains, the red peaks. I fixed my eyes on the metallic wing of the plane, and I let the buzzing of the propellers put me to sleep, but I never could remember the faces of the passengers who traveled with me.

When it grew dark, I returned to Tijuana, letting the bike glide downhill gently, with a certain rhythm, by inertia. Another afternoon had gone by, but it was not the last. A few days later I watched the bimotor Piper Comanche descend, its wings low, appearing in the sky first as an insignificant mosquito. It touched ground without a sound and immediately turned with an extraordinarily fine maneuver into its parking space. I took several pictures.

The woman was accompanied by a man in a sea blue jacket. They went down to the city together, but the next morning the little yellow airplane was no longer parked on the runway. I saw her arrive like that several times, either alone or with someone else. She piloted the airplane. The fact that she knew how to fly a plane made me see in her a power and a superiority that separated her from me irremediably, as if she came from another world and possessed the ability to disappear at will at any time and in any direction.

My airport visits decreased. The photographs that I had been furtively taking disconcerted me as much as their original subject did, but in them I was more likely to see her with pleasure, without fear, and my contemplation could be infinite. Beverly opened the plane door, put her foot on the wing, and lightly jumped to the ground. She wore sunglasses, a silk scarf. Her only baggage seemed to be a canvas sack that she shoved back with her left elbow. The black trimotor, skeletal and propellerless, showed up suddenly in the background of several photographs like a dried-up goose or an eagle with its babies hidden, like the faded photograph from a yellowing newspaper that showed my father and a group of fellow telegraph operators, their arms around each other, at the end of the 1920s, under the loving wing of a trimotor Ford.

My father, with his tobacco-colored mustache, was showing off a pearl-white vest and a grey rabbit-skin hat, and in the background, undefined and out of focus, the tiny airport's control tower stretched upward like a minaret, orchestrating the air taxi service between Hollywood and the Agua Caliente casino. The trimotor Ford had been the sturdy workhorse of the mail service and the intercontinental transportation trade, and it was the same plane that inaugurated diverse routes into formerly inaccessible regions. That tin-plated seagull or goose was shaped like an elongated rhomboid with an aluminum fuselage, three motors inserted into nose and wing, the central motor more prominent than the two lateral ones. It flew practically all the known routes in those days, in the service of both civilian and military companies. It was used for both passengers and cargo. It was amphibious and could land on tires, skis, or pontoons. Almost two hundred trimotor Fords were constructed between 1925 and 1932. Even in Spain, despite the fact that Germany and Italy owned far more sophisticated machines, the first Republican military advances owed much to the legendary trimotors. Even today, some of these artifacts, now reconditioned, continue to fly, uniting distant points of the hemisphere. They have greater take-off power compared to other contemporary planes, and they retain their predecessor's durability: their aluminum skin is light and more weather resistant. Their foot-operated brakes work hydraulically. Their control cables are internal, not external as in earlier models.

A mass of rusted metal squatting alongside a few puddles, the discarded trimotor plane served as a frame to the images, and its worn-out cabin, whose holes my camera's telephoto lens entered, back-shadowed the airport's runway, the barbed wire fence, and Beverly's foot that, little by little, slid down from the airplane's wing, the tips of her toes reaching the ground first, and later, her full body outlined, silk scarf flying backward. Because of the fading light, the last photographs showed nothing but dark splotches, without nuances, illustrations of nothingness: the signaling of an absence, that of the definitive disappearance of the Piper and its passengers, the total abandonment of the airport as a base or merely official customs station.

I could no longer go anywhere because I always carried within me the fear of seeing her suddenly, the terror of finding her again, even if she remained unaware of my body. It didn't prevent me from peeking into the waiting rooms of the airport, even though it seemed too obvious to pretend that I might run into her accidentally, a non-casual gesture that I attempted daily without achieving the desired result. How is it possible to want something so much and at the same time to do nothing to fulfill that desire?

Later on, I resigned myself to giving up this habit. I only watched from afar and from below the control tower, and, by night, gazed at the luminous arm of her reflector as it caressed the clouds. I began inventing itineraries with different routes, heading toward the beach and excluding the hills, and at sunset I found refuge in photography. I set up an easel against one wall indicating my exact height, my perfect posture in terms of how I held my shoulders, my natural inclination, the precise degree of elevation—at a specific height—of my chin. I set up the camera on its tripod facing the easel, set the timer on the automatic shutter release, and took that day's photograph of myself. Afterward, I put up new shelves in the darkroom and locked myself in it for days and nights experimenting with photographic materials. There was a very slight but noticeable difference between one photograph and the next, a barely discernible change taking place each twenty-four hours, the forehead a little shinier sometimes, the fearful gaze, the bitter smile of predictable aging, or the eyebrows a little closer together than the day before. Then I isolated Beverly from the group scenes, rescuing one single detail at a time (a foot, her face in profile, her elbow on the travel bag), and in the foam delayed her path toward the light with the fixant fluid. This isolation provided me with another justification for my curiosity about going out into the streets; it allowed me to recuperate desire and see with another set of eyes. It seemed as if it were only last night, not weeks earlier, that I had searched the area for the last time, in and around the airport and on the golf course greens, although at the same time I had the feeling that I had just arrived from a very long trip. None of the faces I ran into on the street seemed at all familiar to me.

III

Each daybreak restores Beverly to objects and to my first words. Beverly showed up one day at the airport. Beverly moved. Beverly gave me a kiss. Beverly fell at my side in the car when we arrived at the border. All this I can see. It might seem that I no longer find it significant, that time has befogged everything. You have squirrel teeth, I told her. And there she was laughing again, just like a child. She barely reached my shoulder. I hugged her with a natural gesture, without premeditation. One day we watched the sun come up on the beach and we counted one, two, three seconds. The lighthouse beacon flashed on and off every three seconds at first, then every six seconds. I taught her to read Spanish: *Susi. Ésa es Susi. Susi se asea. Así es Susi.* In an unexpected moment, she returned the favor: Pepe is a brave *charro* who lassoed his horse. If you draw the line, as you already know, it is the letter O . . . But I also want her to live, to speak to me, to kiss me, to ask me, How are you, to call me by name, to tell me, Hey,

love, it's been a long time since I've seen you, where in
the world have you been?

No trace of her exact dimensions leaves my hands. My
sketches want to turn her into a splotch and my eyes
imagine in that spot a hidden and unsuspected face. I see
her at twelve years old when, in a white dress and braids,
she raced her bicycle toward the fallen pirul tree until she
was lost to view behind the road's embankment. Perhaps
she continued on through the rocky land and left her bicycle by the fence. The house on the hill. I don't know
more, but I imagine that abstracting her from that nocturnal environment is inevitable. How can I imagine a
flowing river, thermal baths, straggling houses constructed on the outskirts of the city? At that time, Beverly
must have been at least twelve or thirteen years old. Age
doesn't tell you much about a person. She might also have
been the woman sitting in the doorway of her house
watching the children chase each other around, or one of
the young girls who scared dogs away from the little
neighborhood. The suburbs that, little by little, began to
take shape in the scallops of the beach or in the foothills
of the mountains were groupings of broken-up packing
cartons and apple boxes. They were still incomplete as
far as houses go: jury-rigged constructions of rough wood
and slats covered by blackened cardboard, with tarred
roofs and wire fencing nailed to the walls—leftover materials from antiaircraft shelters. It was impossible to recognize her sitting down, contained and unflappable in the
face of screams coming from the sulfur-water baths, or
lying back in the grass at the secondary school. In front
of the house, the trash barrel fires had gone out. Dog families multiplied and hunted hungrily at night. Since there
were no disgusting piles for them to bury their noses in,
the skinny dogs got discouraged in the marshes. Huge

numbers of bony dogs slunk away under the rain of stones thrown by the children. A cow herded by the dogs drowned itself in the false riverbanks.

And then she was someone else—older. She left the Aloha or the Blue Fox Club very early in the morning wearing a green silk dress, after spending the evening with bored sailors or soldiers from San Diego and before feeling the bright sun on her back and running into the icy wind of early October, yearning as never before for clean sheets, a feather pillow, and an afternoon bath. What did it matter that she had a worn face with prominent cheekbones and blonde and chestnut hair? What was essential was her style of being—of really being—and not asking too many questions of herself. It must have come from an elemental strategy for dealing with the world. To whom else would it occur, at that time, to hang out in the riverside cabarets and allow herself to be tempted by dancers or sailors, or to stay out until daybreak in the middle of the street with the pretext that only in this way, watching people pass by from the vantage point of a bench or from the fender of an automobile, could she really get to know the city?

But the streets were question marks. The neon signs, the decorations on a cabaret like the Aloha, were not so much statements as signs of doubt. And it had been forever, because phantasmagorical constructions were now being built that at least attempted to contain two or three authentic walls, more than those of the Hollywood sets offering a picturesque cardboard version of Tijuana, a city of women, of many women of all ages: rivers, rivers of women, dry rivers and sandy basins.

With the hot sun on her shoulders, Beverly escaped from the Aloha and parsimoniously abandoned the north side of the city, weaving among potholes, evil smelling fried food stands, and long lines of cars with license plates from the two Californias. The obscure organization of the river cabarets had been enveloping her ever since her first sporadic visits to the border. In its glory years, the city served as her refuge. Those were the dry years, the years after the closing of the Agua Caliente casino, after World War II, after the Korean War. The city grew outward toward the mountains, living on contraband income from milk and gasoline, from tires and car parts; they swept the dollars up with a broom. Its floating population no longer floated after the wars, and in that way what was a tiny settlement at the end of the last century became a ghost town at first, then a marvelous no-man's-land in which both natives and visitors knew themselves to be lost. Only businesses making an immediate profit survived, and they aspired to industrialize abortion, gambling, entertainment centers, and cheap local handicrafts.

"I'm cold."

By the time the sun has finally made an appearance, I have Beverly's belongings stored in the car.

"I'll drive," I tell her. "You sleep."

IV

I should take her straight to the hangar where the flying instructor waits. I should listen to her without looking at her. Or I should glance at her silhouette against the car window from out of the corner of my eye while driving through the fog with my gaze fixed on the cars in front of me. We were sharing the same seat and, on her side, flowing backward underneath the complex cloverleafs of highways running one against the other, was an enormous cemetery, as befits a city so large, so criminal. On the other side of the window, grass was beginning to appear, one could smell it. The noise lessened. One could reach out and grasp the silence of the cemetery. Brusquely, with the transposition of several gigantic, spherical, nickelized tanks of gas, the mountain became a mesa. The Piper Comanche awaited her. The flying instructor had already warmed up the engines. And I watched them, watched him and her, race up the runway and take off. I watched them lose themselves in the clouds and reappear heading toward the coast. I lost them from sight from the cafeteria where I had gone to wait for her.

Trees and golf courses surrounded the airport to the north. Tennis court fences lay in the distance. The wire fence rose up between me and a large part of the countryside, but, in any case, the lack of a picture window made me a participant in the noises and made me feel the wind current that tugged at the supersonic planes as they changed position and banked into the runway. The earth unstuck itself from the fuselage, was left below, sank away, fell down, separated itself and then came back, little by little, to lightly touch the tires of the airplane. Beverly was at the controls. The old sky wolf proudly taught her to fly. I walked toward the flying field and looked at her. She clambered down from the yellow airplane. She walked tall and laughingly in her tailored suit, the collar left open. Until that very moment I had never realized that the crown of her hair was a thing of beauty, and as she walked closer, with each step I saw her as more alone, less accompanied; she was finally with me. She crossed the entrance hall and upon appearing in the cafeteria doorway, an unlit cigarette in her mouth, walking toward me, she was now completely alone. I had waited for her. I had been contemplating her just as I had planned to do and, as before, we were to meet again many times. We would take each other's hands and we would leave the airport behind forever. We would recognize the same hallways of the night school in the ex-casino, we would stroll around once more from ten o'clock at night until sunrise. And I would awaken, with a tired gesture, with a false gesture of emotion.

Splotches, flowerings, narrow strips separated the city from the ocean. Numerous sand tongues met to form the dunes. On the seaside there were large stretches of quicksand without vegetation. Toward the escarpment and on the hillsides, shrubs and grasses sprouted. A dominating wind intensified during the night and accumulated sand and more sand. The waves punished the dunes, and one could clearly see how their evolution and form depended upon the wind and humidity. Tiny fossil granules stuck to one's feet.

The airplane slipped gently down the improvised beach runway. The Piper Comanche's three feet gave off sparks and buried themselves in the flat, damp sand. Beverly piloted the plane. Later she took off and disappeared. At first she only stayed there during the weekends. She avoided the sea and preferred to walk through the dunes, the transverse coastal sandbanks, parallel and close to the beach, burying her feet in the sand. That quality of earth seemed to attract her.

From the escarpment, at sunrise, one could see more clearly the Piper Comanche parked next to the bungalows. It stood out, tied down to a rock with ropes, the cabin covered with a tarp. The wind shook it slightly. Thus, from afar, I was able to see her more and more often. I saw her enter the bungalow, go out onto the beach, return to shut herself in for a whole weekend, or go up to the airplane, warm up the engines, and disappear. She would arrive on the most unexpected days, and there was no pattern to her trips. The only thing that seemed obvious to me was that the bungalow was her home. She had a way of taking it over and of abandoning it in such a way that no one would take her for a stranger. I still didn't have a name for her, but at the time it was enough for me to know that she lived there and that sometimes she would leave for half of the evening or a couple of hours. It satisfied me to be able to prove that she was as tall as I had always seen her, slim, that she walked aimlessly, that she slept the entire morning away, sometimes sleeping for ten hours, that she rubbed herself with coconut oil when she lay out on the beach. I imagined if I were to touch her at night I would still be able to feel the sun in her warm skin, in her ears, on her lips as she kissed me, and that together we would run along the beach or float in the thick sea. Although during that first stage of our relationship she remained an anonymous being, a distant and inaccessible person who I was limited only to contemplating, I felt that I was living with her.

I woke up speaking to her.

Where in the world had she gone off to? What kind of life did she lead? If she was in some way related to the theater, I could very easily go up to her at the actors' exit or I could just watch her on stage without ever going closer to get to know her. The silence outside terrified me, as did the silence there inside the room. I didn't move. Mutely I looked into each of the corners and at the rug, the dried piñones on the center table, the scant books on the bookshelves. I had never entered further than the living room and the little dining room. The rooms, elon-

gated in shape, led off to one side of the hall. The bedroom. A badly made double bed took up most of the
space. I felt the need to run out of there, but soon I found
myself going into other rooms. There was a playroom
with a television, a chest with sweaters falling out of
drawers and perfume bottles on its top, along with a typewriter, papers, and notebooks. When I opened the closet
I saw several dresses and pairs of women's pants. From
the same horizontal pole hung men's jackets and over-
coats. Below, on top of a suitcase, a wooden box stuck
out, a kind of dark brown trunk.

I asked myself if some day I would ever really make her
acquaintance, if I would run into her and pretend that I
was very pleased to meet her for the first time, even
though I had been hiding in her house and sleeping in
her bed, under her blankets, taking possession of each
and every one of the things her hands had touched. I began to eat at her table. I ate her food, from her dishes:
canned soup, cookies, dates. I cooked on her stove, in her
pots, using her saltshaker. I read her books. I sat for hours
in her bathtub submerged in warm water with a snifter
of cognac by my side. I soaped myself with her bath
brush. I dried myself with her towels. I walked barefoot
through the house. I made myself tea with the tea bags I
found in her pantry. A letter addressed to her and the
electricity bill receipt gave me her real name: Beverly . . .
Now I knew what her name was, Beverly . . . A big straw
basket held utensils, wax fruits, a long and slightly transparent dress, black tights, some clownish high-heeled
shoes with laces, a flannel jacket that I promptly appro-
priated. I learned about her tastes from her record collection. A long, thin brochure, "Private Flying Club of
Southern California," listed air routes, beaches and hotels, and private landing strips on the southern part of the

peninsula. After a few days I began to convince myself that she would be back at any time, that she had only stepped out for a minute. I worried about the possibility of her coming into the house without knocking, using her key to open the door of *her* house, and surprising me asleep in *her* bed.

My hand made a trembling caress. Uncovered, the trunk displayed its internal disorder: a pile of envelopes from the Mexican postal service with green and red lines on the edges. Then some typewritten pages of a probably autobiographical story . . . Several photographs stuck out among the papers. One of them showed a girl posing next to a nice robust woman who was wearing sunglasses— not very dark ones—and a dress with triangular shoulder pads. In another picture the same girl smiled from among a group of girls in uniform. The photographs that looked like they came from a studio were packaged together with a big sheet of proofs: the face was photographed numerous times in the same pose, hair swept up, lips moistened, eyes fixed on the camera—Beverly at fifteen or eighteen, long lashes, slightly plucked eyebrows, unlipsticked mouth. And I could tell that later she had evidently grown precipitously and abruptly; it was traced there in her widely separated eyes, in the lank hair and the tailored suit and the open collar of her white silk blouse. Her gaze hid badly her essential opposition to everything around her, her way of not agreeing to anything. Later on, in another picture, she appeared dressed all in denim, with a heavy shirt and pants, lounging on the patio in the foreground while in the background I could make out an apparently reclusive group of women, and once again Beverly had an unlit cigarette between her lips, a box of matches in her hand.

I couldn't figure out why the envelopes weren't addressed to her, but rather to other people in Santa Monica or San Francisco. The fact is that the letters were written by her, or at least she wrote most of them, the bunch that was in chronological order and tied together with a black ribbon. It seemed she had taken part in a film made in Cabo San Lucas a few years ago and had stayed on to live for a while in Mulegé. Little by little her history began to order itself in my head, despite some fragmentary passages and several incomprehensible allusions that had no apparent connection to each other. It was as if I were watching a movie from the middle, or maybe just isolated clips. I took out the wooden box and set it very carefully on the table next to the typewriter. I tipped it slowly until the letters began to spread out in a memorizable display, so that I would be able to put them back into the box in their original order when the time came. I kept reading each letter through from beginning to end indiscriminately. And I felt that I was on the brink of integrating mentally the plot of anecdotes and names, but there were still some loose threads, some vague references and details that were enough to confuse me even though they seemed to obey a certain logical clarity. I preferred not to know too much. Among the papers I also found a small collection of sepia-colored envelopes and a few others of a Japanese style and workmanship. The first group dealt with food, talking about pork chops in sweet and sour sauce, about glazed duck, about how I love to cook, about entire afternoons spent on the beach, about different kinds of cheese, about wine, he knows some really incredible recipes, yes, four or more times, almost always, at night, just like before, Do you remember?, What a redundancy to say I'm happy. And later, I'll have to leave one of these days. The other night I couldn't escape the inevitable. It was going to happen sooner or later, so I just helped things along and didn't go back to the hotel. But I don't want to talk much about all that. A week later exactly the same thing happened. Only that I never expected him to be so abrupt, so brutal. The relationship is not working out. We've known this has been coming, What do you expect? There is nothing we can do. You can't live in ecstasy all the time and for a lifetime. And he shut up. I would have preferred anything else, an insult, something, for chrissake, he acted like I was scolding him and told me I was right about everything. He didn't defend himself. You'll never amount to anything, I told him, you only go halfway, you never finish anything . . . But for whatever reason, living alone is a very ungenerous option . . .

Later on she met a Japanese actor who was passing through Cabo. She thought he was from Java, she wrote, sort of the idea I had always had of an oriental romance. She talked about the Mulegé beaches, how they were green and silvered underneath, that she would have preferred to arrive after summer was over and she asked her girlfriend (the person to whom she was writing the letter, and almost all the letters in her collection) to loan her some money and some books. This first contact with Beverly's silent and written voice made me read faster. In that instant I saw periods and commas and couldn't figure out how I was able to decipher her handwriting so easily. I jumped quickly from one letter to another. It turned out to be impossible for me to link together people and places mentioned only in passing. As I read from one paragraph to another, an Italian name stood out: she spoke about him as if he were her husband, or as if she saw him every day, and mentioned him in almost all the letters. Afterward the references to Luciano were chilly; still later the tone was one of absolute repudiation. But not all the letters were organized by dates; some followed the others with a difference of about ten days, still others preceded the first ones I read. They lived in Mulegé, but they had gone to spend a few days in Cabo San Lucas. There appeared to have been an argument, an irreconcilable misunderstanding, and they broke up. Apparently Beverly had wandered off one of those nights and hadn't come back until the next morning. In a tight, tense handwriting she confided in her girlfriend that she was going to have a baby, but, later on, in a short typewritten letter, she brought up the possibility of preventing it. There was also a note, written on a napkin, about a conversation that she had in a Cabo café, etc., etc.

At a certain point I began to lose interest. I was bored with the fragmentary snapshots of the letters. Her desire to keep them, for who knows what reasons, the fact of accumulating objects to remind her of the past, impoverished the ideal image that I wanted to have of her. I looked over each of the photographs again, I almost spoke to her right to her face, I felt deeply within myself that we had known each other for many years. With the same caution as I had used in the beginning, I returned the whole pile of papers to the box and put it back in the closet. I was trembling when I caught a glimpse of myself in the dressing table mirror, I smoothed down my hair with my hands, I avoided looking at myself straight in the eyes. I only dared glance at my face for a brief instant, out of the corner of my eye, or with my chin on my chest. Then I worried for a few moments about checking over the room to make sure it was left exactly as I had found it. There was some underwear hanging from the shower head: a black bra, some nylon pantyhose. The same Formica table in the kitchen. I made a gesture of farewell in the emptiness.

Without raising her voice, Beverly offered me a piece of candy, a mint egg, and for the first time I saw that she was dressed in white. She looked younger than she was. The connecting walls resonated with the voices of older people. She had the air of a recently married woman; then she took on the appearance of a girl of twelve or thirteen with her hair pulled up, her face clean, and she almost reached my eyelids. She was lying on the cot when we were on the brink of kissing each other for the first time, but the cascading voices in the background stopped us. Beverly sucked on a lemon and lay back almost horizontally on the canvas-covered lawn chair. We were afraid. I was terrified of the idea that someone might shoot a rifle from above us in the hills, someone who felt like killing someone. A patch of tiny insects spread underneath the lawn chairs. They were silver, like little metal tubes. Someone commented that they were locusts and, sure enough, the insects started to eat the potted plants, leaves, earth. Suddenly I saw that they were eating the Spanish rice spilled on the ground. I got a bottle of turpentine to exterminate the plague, but it was futile; I filled my mouth with it and then spit it out on the bugs. Uselessly.

"I am what I can be. I am what I can be. Kill me then . . . I am whatever you believe me to be. I am what others believe me to be. I am whatever the rest want me to be."

"Get out of here," she told me. "Go someplace where they are making new countries every day, do something, for good or ill, but do something. Wake up from your apathy," she insisted, exasperated. Afterward, she looked at me. "Go to the corner and buy an ice-cream cone."

She threw a five-cent coin at me, I caught it in the air, and I ran to buy the ice-cream cone and returned to share it with her, to lick the scoop of ice-cream together. I felt like her accomplice, squandering together, secretly, the small amount of household money, without inviting anyone to share.

"The dunes are tongue-shaped," she said. "They reshape themselves behind any obstacle, any windbreak."

She spoke to me of other beaches, of a weekend she spent alone in the south. She was dressed in a terry cloth robe and she had taken off her false eyelashes. She wore her hair pulled back. Next to the bed the hole of the mirror transfigured her absent face, making her overlap with another world. Each of her movements blocked off a hurtful memory, as did her silences, the dead times, and the irreplaceable broken-off happiness. Without ever seeming to get to the point, she held back her words, she drowned in the ineluctable contemplation of the drawings of superimposed bodies and intertwined legs that adorned the headboard of her bed, the fragmented self-portrait, the vacuum emanating from certain objects that lacerated her. And it was true: in no part of herself had she been able to reconstruct the best of her life as discovered in other beings. Those days on the beach slipped by without a single night in which she could sleep well.

She seemed to want to tell me that there is no woman with a clean past, that she was someone who had been marked forever by other hands, that there was something fatally irrecoverable in her.

In vain she eluded references to herself, unable to go

back to the beginning of her tale until the weighty silence of the room defeated her.

"It's a place that has all these cottages for ships' captains," she continued. "Miniature brigantines and galleons, and there, in that place of bungalows and of umbrellas planted in the sand, I walked alone, with no one else around. It was enough for me to slip on the dunes, those reaches of prickly sand, far away from the sea foam and the rocks. I could have thrown myself in with my clothes on, without thinking twice. I was in the middle of the sandbanks. Soon I felt the water at my ankles, but I didn't even have to dampen the tips of my toes to realize that the sand was thickening, despite the sun, despite the definitive end of winter. There were a lot of dunes, with almost vertical slopes. I didn't know what to do, so I took off my clothes. The beach was abandoned, not a soul in sight, no one. I let myself fall, burying my feet. As I descended, the sand turned damp, and soon my feet were hidden in a puddle. I never wanted you to come with me because at that time I wanted to be alone and not speak with anyone. I undressed. I put my outfit on a sandy slope—it was a very pretty orange palazzo pajama suit. It hardly took up any volume. I began to get cold, so then I took a picture of the shape that the palazzo pajama took, half filled with small lumps of sand. In that moment, even with my slightly faded white silk slip, I felt that I was dressed in an ancient Greek tunic, and I took all twelve pictures from that roll of film of my poor, beloved dress with the wide shoulder pads that was not, after all, the palazzo pajama that I mentioned. I was very alone, just as I liked to be. And now I feel under my feet this bit of sea and I feel the breeze. I contemplate the night and my lungs take control of the salty wind. But, at any rate, you ought to have come with me. I would have taken you to

see the salt flats, the rivers that feed into the sea, to eat
smoked fish and dried fruit. Someday we'll go to see those
places together: the missions, the orchards. Those were
the years when your father was as old as you are now.
They were fabulous years. I loved the double-breasted
suits like the one your dad wore, the feathered hats, the
patent-leather shoes. I loved seeing Rita Cansino's debut
in the Agua Caliente casino, hearing about Jean Harlow's
Tijuana lover, betting on the roulette board and rolling
the dice, watching the sunrise from the Salón de Oro ter-
race. I was delighted with people like Isadora Duncan,
not to be a dancer twenty-four hours a day, to find and
express a new way of life, to begin a party in Paris, continue it in Venice, and conclude it weeks later on a yacht
floating down the Nile, to spend three thousand dollars
on lilacs, to want to see Zelda Fitzgerald, the southern
lady, scandalizing New York on top of pianos or crossing
Fifth Avenue on the roof of a taxi with Scott, to die of a
moonmadness. But why yearn for something we know
nothing about? It hurts me to tell you this, but you can't
do anything for me. I'm the one who's sick. There was a
moment when I was no longer with you. But I swear it's
nothing. It's not that. No, it's not that either. I can't believe it; I don't want to believe it. There was a time when
I no longer felt anything. Like a dead woman. Why do we
never coincide? You, after all, have not been the most
important thing in my life."

V

We stopped seeing each other, and it was as if each of us
had buried the other. From that time on, coinciding with
a somber and rainy sunrise, the only thing that united us
was silence; not heat or insomnia, not the drowsiness we

fell into because of the noises on the escarpment near the bungalow, noises captured in the absorbent materials of walls and halls formerly inhabited by other beings. The creaking of the staircase reflected, beyond a doubt, the footsteps that another man impressed upon them, many years ago and throughout many years, as he entered and left, as he constructed, day by day, his happy conviviality with that house. Somehow the objects retained his body, his humors, his feelings. He remained there like a tender and beloved ghost. The cat went to the door and meowed in its sad search for him. But now the footsteps corresponded to my feet; I went downstairs with no hope but that of my definitive expulsion toward the beach, the breech, the highway, the first streets of the city still barely traveled by the strolling street vendors who offered passersby grapefruit juice while tired and chilly men and women huddled at the bus stop on the corner. An old man arranged the morning papers in his kiosk. Life was reborn, with all the cruelty of a foggy atmosphere that canceled out any luminous possibility, almost certainly in the same instant in which she, free once again, closed the door, locked it, felt a weight lift from her, put on her bathrobe, and climbed into bed to awaken at sunset.

We had been living from afternoon to afternoon, from night to night, in the house that was temporarily ours. There was a beveled-glass door at the top of the stairway and in it we drew the shapes of Gothic church windows. From the balcony I used to look down onto the circular park eternally surrounded by cars that raced past the fountains, benches, and couples. I climbed on top of the coffee table and raised my arms as if I were about to improvise a speech. I imagined myself trembling in front of the microphone, in front of a crowd into whose faces I dared not look directly. I tried to find the words and the gestures and stuttered irrelevant phrases. I practiced my speech to myself or I thought it aloud. I talked to the walls. Ceremonies had taken place there that would never be repeated. Before long we came together. We learned every detail of our bodies, each and every movement, and we always, always found new ritual versions. Her breath, her saliva, her tongue transmitted the fragrance of the interior flesh that shapes itself into bodies. We were one single animal with doubled extremities. We scattered newspapers and orange towels on the floor. She dozed off while I began to paint the walls white. We covered up our clothes with plastic bags. I began painting in the corners and the window frames. I carefully rubbed off the old, peeling paint with a rag dipped in gasoline. In some places the paint gave way to lime and I could hear how the gasoline penetrated the walls and burned them. I fell asleep next to her.

The sunlight coming in the window awakened me. I sat up on the edge of the bed. I watched her sleep, her hair tangled, her face half-hidden in the pillow. When I got up and circled the bed, looking for my clothing, I felt her gaze upon me. Smiling at her, I went closer and stood by her side. She touched me between my legs and took me into her right hand. Slowly, she seemed to nibble at me, and my penis grew as her lips widened. In and out with her eyes closed, her hair lost between my legs. I felt her palate, then a soft suction, I was lost, coming as if I had lost my skeleton, deboned and searching for her. When I dropped to her side I lowered myself to the height of her mouth. I kissed her. Upon opening my eyelids, I saw that she was gazing directly into my eyes. I entered her as if she were the extension of my own eyes in the mirror. I did not ponder her pupils or the color of her irises or the white globes of her eyes. It wasn't her eyes that I was looking at. Or maybe I wasn't looking at anything. I went into her as if I were exploring all of her, inhabiting her, not feeling her as a part of myself but rather as a world that had always been in her and with her, with all of her past and her way of seeing things and interpreting my words, a world, her world, that began with infancy and slowly, through time, became present and inescapable to me. It didn't matter to me that I didn't know her exact landscapes, the other periods of her life, her past sufferings, or her fugitive joys. Separate from me, I nevertheless recognized myself in her, in a transparent composition that confused or reforged our bodies and faces, making us one and contrasting us, not only the skin-to-skin contact, but also her smells, the fragrance of her hair as she left the bathroom the night before, all the internal fluids released between our two shaking bodies. She had wrapped a towel on her head like a turban when she came out of the steamy shower, dripping.

"The water is really cold," she told me. "How do you turn on the hot water?"

So then I turned on the hot water faucet and she was enveloped in steam.

"That's really bad for your circulation," I warned her. But she preferred boiling water falling on the nape of her neck.

"Women always stand with their back to the shower," she told me. "We don't face forward. Men always bathe frontward, with their face against the stream of water so it massages their facial muscles."

"You're going to cook," I told her. "Like a chicken."

She emerged from the steam, with her turban on her head like an Islamic princess, looking for more towels.

"Why do you want so many towels? You're such a maniac. One for your feet, another for your back. Another for your head. Another for your face."

"No matter how many I use, there is always a drip left that later shows up on my blouse."

Afterward we ate nuts. We had to walk carefully when we got up and had to reach for our clothes while avoiding nutshells. She turned around without saying anything. She turned her back to me and we didn't speak again until we had watched the whole afternoon pass by, seated in the canvas lawn chairs and seeing how the sea blended with the fog. But in that moment of sudden muteness I did not have the feeling, not even the vague suspicion, but rather the absolute certainty that Beverly had never lived with me. Never, not at any moment, not in any sense, not even for a brief friendship. I was left with my empty arms, idiotized, screaming like a Roman tribune on top of the table. What kind of monologue or dialogue was I inventing with myself? It bothered me not to be able to verify whether or not the stay in that room had anything at all to do with the Beverly that arrived at the airport, with that woman with the big, widely spaced eyes and mussed hair, with the tailored suit and the open collar, the unlit cigarette in her mouth, the matches in her hand . . . What caused the anger that furrowed her brow? Where did that fundamental rebelliousness burst from, that complex and difficult contradiction?

At that time they had spoken to me about the violence in the city. Police squadrons patrolled the corners. Troops in the streets. Ominous foreboding. Streetlights were scarce and the nights were very long. Arriving at the bungalow door didn't offer me any relief; the dangerous ascension of the stairway or the probable encounter with a hand and a knife still mediated. The only refuge was upstairs, after opening the door with the Gothic window-panes and closing it with various padlocks. It was the only safe place in the whole world, the spot she loved, she whose indefatigable hands had imposed order on the bookshelves, the bathroom, the closets, the kitchen. Her personal belongings were scattered everywhere. The first time I entered, exhausted, I stared at the furniture without noticing details. I was terrified that someone might break in, kicking down the door, or that someone might stare in through one of the windows and surprise me. I unplugged the refrigerator so that I could eliminate the humming of the motor and could wake up with the least amount of strange noise.

But after that fantasized internment, after that simulacrum of new and good intentions, I saw her get out of a taxi, pass by the stands selling oranges and slices of watermelon in the market, saw her pause in a vacant lot full of discarded peelings and bits of garbage when I photographed her. She ran barefoot toward the back of the house and collapsed on the rug, went into the shower, cleaned the car's windshield dirtied from a rainy Sunday on the highway, straightened out the records in their cases, drowned with silence the blush of inopportune evocations surging from the music, from the old Jacques Brel album, from Greta Keller's "pian pian piano in the next apartment," looked distastefully at the splotched self-portrait, at the illegible calligraphic designs, touched the objects worn down by innumerable hands.

I saw her get out of a taxi and I began to follow her. It was sometime in the afternoon, that indefinite, sweet sequence of minutes in the twilight that precedes full night. And she entered into that night. She crossed the boulevard, began to walk faster, unconsciously allowed me to glimpse the canvas bag, the silk scarf, the flannel jacket, and her hair: blonde and chestnut, blonde and chestnut. I hurried forward at the very second in which I identified her by her back; I brought my hands to my mouth in a megaphone and could barely whisper, enchanted, her name. But gradually I fell silent. I shortened the footsteps that were bringing me closer to her. I remained ecstatic, frozen in place, and I let my quarry go . . . Beverly reached the edge of the crosswalk, jumped up onto the sidewalk, began to stroll, sure of herself, with a clearly fixed goal, with a precise route, down the sidewalk opposite the one on which I was walking with my vision fixed to one side, focused on her. Benches and trees interposed themselves ahead. I imagined that she would pick up her car, which must be parked on one of the corners. Beverly passed by without paying any attention to the rows of black cars lining the street. She did not go into the building located next to the big park; she followed the rhythm of her own footsteps without slowing down. Trailing her forced me into an uncontrolled animal movement. In contrast with my body, which moved among the passersby, avoiding them by reflex, my paralyzed icy face, eager for her, was irresistibly attracted to the unmistakable leaps of the gazelle who continued onward along the street's left sidewalk. I pursued her obliquely with my gaze. I imagined myself the hero in a cinematic spy scene. Suddenly, as my visual field was crowded by billboards, illuminated signs, lampposts, trees, cars, couples walking hand in hand, bicycles, and buses, the streets became an impersonal and monstrous crowd. I caught sight of her again behind a newspaper stand. As we both moved forward, the park's walkway separated us. I could make her out through the streams of water and the mist of the fountain. She turned the corner. I ran after her. I found her again. I stopped: I was getting too close. I allowed her to go on ahead. The great park curved in a trajectory parallel to both of us. I gave free rein to my prey. Beverly crossed the street diagonally. A corner hid her. The intersection of two streets prevented me from finding her. I thought I saw her disappear behind the door of a beauty parlor. I was afraid of confusing her with another woman who furtively entered a hotel. I felt my stomach cramp when I confirmed that no, there was no one in the dark alleyway. I saw a medical clinic, a parking lot, clothing stores, cafés with empty tables on the sidewalk. My eyes searched back and forth in the windows of the apartment building. I had lost her from sight definitively. I went back the way I had come, retracing my steps, only mine, mine without hers, with damp hands, with nothing to offer or to offer myself. I was downcast with an incomprehensible and deliberately sought pain, dead of fear and trembling with the cutting preference for choosing doubt over a pleasurable encounter followed by a spontaneous greeting, a casual street meeting.

I followed the same street back, passing under the fountain's mist, waiting until the cars had gone by to cross the street, and I heard her once again telling me that no one is free from the past, pass me the sugar; I once again heard her reconsider her life as discovered in other lives, I have to go, waking up at midnight beside her, we'll meet again someday, sharing the drowsy daydream of an irreplaceable broken-off happiness, watching her take off her false eyelashes, lift up her hair, hearing her say, I'm dead-tired, in front of the hole of a mirror that transfigured her absent face still adhering to another world, seeing her read in the silent living room, arranging the shelves in the emptiness of the study, or watching her cry at the table, for no particular reason, telling her how incomprehensible everything was during those last few days, how tightly closed were the shadows in the trees. What years these last have been, years in which we haven't seen each other, what a temporal disjunction, what a lack of coincidence in our respective instants, hearing her murmur, you, after all, have not been the most important thing in my life, not answering her, deciding never to see her again, arranging without achieving an entirely socially justifiable meeting, writing her letters that end up in the sewer, following her down the line of recently dug graves and flowerless tombs without stones, through empty fields where the boys from the outskirts of town used to play basketball, seeing her get out of a taxi, cross the boulevard, crush the flowers, and slip away into the night.

VI

Hers were the first breasts I ever saw. Beverly was fourteen years old and I was more than fourteen and I lived in the maid's room of a big old white house, segregated like a rabid animal. I painted and repainted my bicycle and attached colored lights all over its body. I scraped it down before painting it again with spray paint: one day orange, the next purple, another day white. After a time the bicycle was left stuck in a corner and the rubber tires rotted. It had once been my sole object of adoration; with it I adventured beyond the prohibited confines of the city, up into the dirt roads and the highways that lead to the airport and to the sea. It was like a secret white goddess, a miraculous being that kept me from being converted into a domesticated man—one of those men locked away between walls, stuck in his shell—since the bicycle was the only means I had to defend myself against the homey world of women and the gangs that terrorized the neigh-

borhood. I heard gossip about the all-out battles that
sometimes polished off the nocturnal basketball games;
I learned of Zambo's death, kicked to dust in a parking
lot. Some of my schoolmates had been left behind on Pacific beaches, in Normandy, in Korea, and in Vietnam,
and it wasn't unusual to see the well-known olive green
car drive up in a cloud of dust from the naval base in San
Diego on its way to the mountains where it would dis-
gorge some admiral or other officer. The mother would
accept without much ceremony the Purple Heart or whatever other posthumous metal she was given for the son
killed on the battlefield.

I never wanted to take part in those particular lives.
Any accidental knowledge I had barely disturbed me and
it surrounded me with desperate conjectures, perhaps because the environment I lived in didn't change much with
the passage of time and because others, not I, were the
real protagonists of those triumphs and tragedies. I tried
to take part, to take on the night and the streets boldly,
but in vain. I'd pass by the riverside cabarets sometimes,
now dark and without clients looking into them one by
one. Sometimes, as the master of ceremonies of the Waikiki, I would announce Rosa Carmina's show ("Yes, siiir!
Rosa Carmina! Greatest ballerina from Mexico City!"),
and in the doorway, at the entrance to the club, I'd warm
up the crowds ("Take a look inside, folks! No cover
charge. The showison, the show is on!"), until that night
in which someone confronted me with disgust and threw
a silver coin in my direction, a coin that fell into the bowl
of the spittoon . . . I knelt down and stuck in one hand to
rescue the silver dollar from the spit.

After that I kept to myself more. The maid's room con-
stituted the perfect spot for self-enclosure. According to
the unchangeable family verdict, there was no hope for

me; I was condemned to spend the rest of my life on top of the house. From morning to night I felt walled up inside a white castle surrounded by darkness. It was the safest spot, unexpungeable, my only refuge, and, by a providential bit of territorial good luck, it was the best lookout point in the area. It dominated the whole neighborhood; it was an observatory designed according to the four cardinal points, just like a fort. In the distance I could see the crisscrossings on the hills while the long, wormlike train slid along like a firefly, climbing the hills in a spiral and boxing them in. Once in a while Beverly was able to sneak in with me and cry, paralyzed with fright, in my arms. We looked at each other.

Beverly peeked in from the embankment every now and again, less and less often as time went on, and she greeted me with a smile.

After several weeks I decided to go out, almost always at night. I tried to wander through the dark alleyways, to peek into the cabarets from far away, to sit down in the garbage dump next to the cliff and try to clarify once and for all if those were the same places that showed up under my open window, on the other side of the thicket and the fallen pirul tree. I walked on, leaving the residential area behind me, while everyone else, at least at that time and in that space, was peacefully asleep.

My old Navy pea jacket with golden buttons protected me from the cold. I wanted to figure out what I could glimpse about those moments just before dreaming and see if they had anything to do with the voices and with the trees in which Beverly liked to hide. I looked myself over from head to toe. I recognized my outfit and freely accepted that underneath the sheets, a few seconds or minutes ago, I had taken off all my clothes, and I only needed to corroborate the fact suggested in the infinite depths of my closed eyes and in the nape of my neck buried in the pillow. I caressed the realization uncovered in that instant when control gently, sweetly escapes toward darkness. I wanted to court it, to save it for myself and not share it with anyone, but only to the degree that the feeling of playing with each one of my visions as I began to fall asleep might signify the incessant repetition of my most intimate and depressing history, the same story reiterated from the beginning, the sudden encounter with everything that I lived or believed I lived from my childhood on and which in that very instant seemed to be concentrated on Beverly's fading silhouette as she ran on the beach or mutely opened her legs next to the sulfur-water baths.

I noticed the smell of locked-up places under the jacket. I could still hear the squeal of the rooftop door; the room was wind-scoured . . . I sat down to smoke on the first log I saw, after buttoning up the jacket and feeling the initials of my father's name on the golden buttons. For a moment I forgot about my search for Beverly. I had the feeling that my father crossed in front of me once again, along the same cliffside path, like an apparition. Before his figure was lost in the descent, I saw him nail the tin numbers on the front of our house with a hammer. He submissively did all the handyman work, made his own dinner, changed the water in the bottles of olives before they spoiled, hauled the drowned cat out of the toilet with a cord, and then he took off down the hill with hurried steps, huddled in his jacket. Sailors and taxis surrounded the hillside house on the outskirts of Tijuana. The night my father took off, I crouched on the ground. I saw the yellow-and-white-painted gate, the sharply aligned posts that supported the ornamental ironwork, and between them I could make out the plants bunched in the patio, the dirty olive tree and the slimy black olives smashed on the ground.

The idea of heading toward the prohibited parts of town had always seduced me, but at that moment I remained immobile on the log, all alone, feeling tempted to wander off on the same pathways my father had taken. Sitting on the log, smoking, my arms brushing against the buttoned chest of the jacket, I looked toward the hilltops and the sheet metal shack next to the tracks. The cargo train passed by and penetrated into the heights, disappearing as if it had been swallowed up by the geological composition of the mountains. I walked toward the cliff and I felt myself to be surer, calmer, when I realized that no one was trying to see me at that hour of the night. The dusty road ended at the sheet metal hut. I walked forward, throwing pebbles against the broken chunks of earth in the dried-up riverside. The hut and the oil tanks took on more and more concrete shapes. I threw a stone at the house and no one answered. Inside the hut rusted bits of iron fell down; against one wall instead of a stove there was a stain of burned wood, and high above swung the switchman's dirty cap. The ground shone blackly with oil. When it became totally dark, the urgency to have Beverly with me once again reemerged fully. It was hard to disabuse myself of the notion that she might be hiding nearby, but even then I was able to calm myself down. I crossed my arms and felt the warmth of my body; I touched each and every one of my ribs, I touched my hips, and curled up in one of the corners of the hut I contemplated my toes. The darkness and the squeaking metal sheets didn't bother me. No one spied on me, not even Beverly. I stayed there for a long time with my gaze fixed upon the hairy extremities of my body. I felt myself growing chilled. I enjoyed the cold silence of the hut. I walked back up the train track. No noise. There were no lights, no trains. Balancing on the track I lifted my arms like wings. I looked to one side and a woman with exposed thighs stepped into a puddle. Beverly lay back on the grass, stretched out like an iron statue. She offered me a ten-dollar bill, and then a piece of candy . . . her fingertips brushed my forearm. She wasn't wearing shoes; she dropped the towel that barely covered her body, she took off the false eyelashes, she dried off feet that had been wrinkled by the water. And upon clambering down the little hill in the road, she ordered me:

"Dress up like a Greek, like a warrior."

I put on a tin breastplate.

"Take off your shoes."

I threw my shoes to one side.

"How marvelous it would be to have golden slippers!"

" . . ."

"I can hear thumpings in your chest: they're heart bubbles."

I lifted her in my arms. I lay her back against the grass, among the geraniums. Beverly smiled less each time, tender, warm, and then . . . frozen. She was no longer with me.

Sadness and the heavy pea jacket chained me to the ground in front of the small, lit valley. A few distant noises barely reaffirmed to some degree the city's presence. The house stood out, white against the pirul trees. I raised the jacket's collar as I began to distance myself further from that vision. Trees and orchards disappeared as I began to walk beneath the embankment toward the mountaintop because up there, on the peak, I could feel that I was closer to the airplanes.

VII

On the backs of their jackets they had embroidered the figure of a winged horse leaping through the clouds, along with letters spelling out the word "Pegasus." They took off their red jackets with white leather sleeves only on exceptional occasions, for example, when they climbed onto the shoulders of the fountain satyr that spit water from its mouth, or when they lay out in the sun at the Agua Caliente casino pool: cynical intruders and singular owners of that space. One of them flew from the diving board, extending his arms and falling without splashing a single drop from the greenish surface of the pool. He dove again, and again repeated the fabulous crucifix upon throwing himself into the air. At the moment in which he disappeared underwater, I impulsively got to my feet and walked toward the diving board. I grabbed the stair railings with both hands and very cockily began to climb, showing off my skinny and curved muscles and my orange swimsuit. I tightened the strings on my suit and looked down: tiny little beings, dwarfs, insignificant ants, sleeping beasts on the lawn; the Pegasuses kept silent and watched incredulously as I calmly dominated the high board. They were stupefied by the sun, some on the benches, others playing around or licking popsicles under the palm trees. All of them were on their stomachs or face up. The guy that had made the spectacular dive had already gotten out of the water and was defiantly beginning to dry himself with whatever towels came to hand. A line of divers were waiting their turns on the diving board immediately beneath the high board from which the Pegasus had thrown himself . . . And a second later I was flying through the air with my arms extended like Christ on the cross, but suddenly I flipped over, felt my feet go up, my head down, my waist arch, and the solid block of green water smashed against me. Those who were laying out on the grass jumped up right away so as not to miss out on any gory detail, any chance to make fun of me. First came the smiles and the saliva dripping out of open mouths, and then came the total and obstreperous belly laughter. And there I was: just about to get them all wet, halfway out of the water, with an indifferent expression on my face and the skin on my legs all reddened, the absolute focus of public attention in the middle of the ex-casino's swimming pool, without the strength or the desire to lift my arms. I barely made it to the mosaic-covered edge. As soon as I got myself upright on the slippery deck and started to walk away, I slipped and fell on my back, slamming my head against the ground, and the pain in my head seemed to spill out my nose. My back burned and my nasal passages felt half-buried. I rinsed my hair and dried myself off with someone's shirt, which I found on the first step of the stairway when I sat down. A cloud covered part of the sun and I got goose bumps. Right away I got to my feet and headed back toward the diving board. Someone stopped me in time, grabbing me by the shoulders and hauling me back with both arms to sit me affectionately down on the step again. Someone else rubbed my neck. They gave me some alcohol to sniff, and a few minutes later I put on my shirt without an undershirt, pulled on my pants over the top of my wet swimsuit, and I took off, without combing my hair, walking along the train tracks and later on through the dry riverbed. I began to climb up the slightly inclined dike. Far away, over the invisible sea, a column of black smoke lifted majestically. Something had caught on fire . . . A firefighter with a red cape and a black helmet swung into a red helicopter as if he were mounting a horse; instead of a Don Quixote lance he carried a hose that squirted out a stream of water at high pressure. He flew above the black cloud, and when he barely got close to it, he went backward and forward, and later disappeared into the surrounding clouds. A combined passenger/cargo ship was burning. The shipwrecked people rowed desperately; they jumped out of their life rafts, leaping for the pier, but instead of a pier there was a huge carpet of plants, fingers, and submerged bodies spread out like a fleshy wharf surface in the shallowest part of the coast.

"Cut!" yelled someone. "Cut! That's it for the day."

I walked forward into the midst of the crowd of actors, actresses, and extras.

"But I'm not an extra," I told them, and I walked over the finger-carpet. I submerged my toes in the thick water. The carpet was a woman's body, a body laying on its back, making me slip. I kissed the woman's breasts; she kissed me back. I thought she might be pretending, and between our conjoined lips was caught a lock of blonde and chestnut hair.

As soon as I came into contact with her, everything fell apart, everything seemed to dislocate itself into thousands of colors and to resonate with innumerable, almost inaudible, noises and vibrations. I never went back to how I was. Thus I felt that I was tiptoeing with great care over the peninsula's veins, as if I were traveling over a blue-tinged and living body, full of branching nerves, rivers, pathways, just like the distribution of the spinal nervous system. And through all of this, obviously, taking extreme measures to set down my toes carefully so as not to awaken this fleshy, flowing surface.

Just before I got home I saw a car accident in the street. The neighbor lady who had once given me a pair of shoes was arguing anxiously with a police officer. I gazed at everyone without interest. I went into the house and went straight to the kitchen. The unfinished model plane still sat on the table: a fish skeleton and wooden-slat wings next to a tube of glue, some China paper, and aeronautical engineering maps. I warmed up some lunch. It started to get dark and I gulped big spoonfuls of soup while I listened to the coffee heating up. I looked out the window of the house and someone screamed. It was the same neighbor who had once given me some patent-leather shoes, and she was very beautiful. I was looking for a cup to put the coffee in when I heard the siren of an ambulance drawing near. The sound buzzed in my ears, although after a bit it began to diminish gradually and faded out in the foothills of the mountains where the train crossed, roaring, every night. And I vomited.

I woke up hours later. I lifted my head from the China paper and shoved aside all the pieces of semiconstructed airplanes. I heard voices in the alleyway. By this time it had nothing to do with the scandal caused by the neighbor woman. And by now nobody was bothering to comfort her or to rescue her. People ran around and mumbled to each other; they talked about the police, about the German family that had been arrested. All along the alley and back toward the cliff a large group of women and children headed toward the German family's house with buckets and jars. An overpowering perfume fragrance permeated the whole neighborhood. People stuck bottles, jars, cans, basins, and coffeepots under the sewer pipe to catch the stream of perfume that burst out. Several police officers broke demijohns in the back patio and the liquid spilled over the mosaic-covered floor and ended up in the pipe that poured out into the alley. The stink of adulterated perfume diffused and began to make the neighbors dizzy . . . I kept on watching the women from my window. Then

I went back to concentrating on the half-built model plane. Little by little it got darker, but I didn't notice the exact moment when night fell. I studied the Spitfire's instructions. I had to apply some British insignia that I didn't have. I got my second wind and made a sketch of the letters "RAF." I thought about the spectacle I put on at the casino's pool, and the Pegasuses' laughter, and the long walk along the dry riverbed and between the train tracks counting the cross-ties, and the branches of the fallen pirul tree, and how hungry I was that afternoon. Much later that night lights went off next door, all except for the back end of the house. From the table I could see someone moving around in the bedroom behind the blinds. I kept on watching her, watching the neighbor who had once given me a pair of shoes. She undressed nervously. She was slim. I couldn't make out her face. I dropped the paper and scissors wherever they happened to fall on the table. I could neither continue cutting nor recuperate the time that I might have been using to sleep. When the neighbor woman came toward the near side of the half-open Venetian blinds, I hurried to shut off the lights. And I saw her. Her nude body was reflected in the mirror. At that very moment, a hand emerged from below, from the lower edge of the window frame, and she took it in hers, leaning back and then disappearing beneath the horizontal lines of the Venetian blinds. It was impossible to continue gluing paper and giving shape and polish to bits of balsa wood. I could make out the neighbor's window again while I cleaned the glue off my hands. But I couldn't see anything else. All I could perceive in the darkness was the outline of the tablecloth and the cut papers, the strips of wood, the plastic and rubber tires, the maps of the peninsula, the aerial navigation charts, the instruction sheets like architectural blueprints, the model airplanes. The Spitfire's box had a color illustration of the Battle of Britain, and it advertised a series of Hurricanes, Mustangs, Messerschmidts, and Tigersharks on one side of the box. The Spitfire's aerodynamic lines blended into the picture along with those of the Hurricane and Japanese Zero planes, and I could see various folds of cinnamon-colored China paper sticking out of one of the boxes, ready for gluing onto the armature I had been working on all summer. I looked at the Flying Tiger squadron lined up on the bookshelves. The Japanese Zero fighters with their sun flags were my headboard planes, with their red and yellow suns on the sides and the little stars-and-stripes pennants that the samurai pilot collected for his combat record. In those days the Japanese planned to slip under the peninsula in a submarine so they could safely attack from the Sea of Cortés. They had been digging a secret tunnel and the final battle would come from beneath us. They would torpedo the military bases in the Colorado canyons, in the Arizona deserts, and they would bomb training camps in Jacumba, Point Loma, the Boeing factories, and the San Diego naval base. They said that the Japanese would arrive by land and by sea, that they would surround the San José del Cabo coasts if the tunnels failed, and they would be the terror of the Gulf of California. In future years we would only eat rice. But later on the enemy would carry the opposing markings. The antiaircraft defense force would knock down three B-52 bombers and four of the Phantom F-111 hunter-seekers with their folding wings. Their crews would be driven to Rumorosa and summarily shot. Throughout the night, one air-raid siren after another would scream its warning. The hunter-seekers would frequently fly over the city at a low altitude, and each explosion would shake the whole downtown area.

Despite the resumption of bombing, however, the attackers would not be able to shake the population out of its traditional astounding bravery and calmness. Without any loss of reflexes, adults and children would line up in front of the collective and individual air-raid shelters when the sirens began to sound the alert, and they would get into them as soon as the first explosions started. A bomb would fall on a movie theater packed with people. The explosion and the collapse of the building would kill nine people and wound another one hundred. Other bombs would damage the already-hit civilian hospital. The most violent attack would come at daybreak. In many of the destroyed houses one would find fragments of women's and children's bodies. The aggressors would launch successive waves of planes, including the B-52s, with the goal of flattening many densely populated sectors of the city and exploding the Rodríguez Dam. The antiaircraft defense force would fight back with earth-to-air missiles. The pride of the North American air force, the B-52, would weigh almost 218 tons and would measure 56 meters from wingtip to wingtip, 48 meters in length, and 12 meters in height. Its maximum velocity would be 1,200 kilometers per hour even when it attacked from an altitude of 12,000 meters, and it would have a range of 14,000 kilometers. Its six crew members would have very specialized technical training, but they would never be able to see the targets upon which they would drop their bombs. The bomber would be furnished with a complex and supersecret electronic instrumentation panel. Seven and a half million tons of bombs would force the capitulation of the strategic superfortresses in the downtown area and in the hills that surrounded the city. Years later the antiaircraft shelters would be only a tangle of chicken wire and twisted metal.

The next morning, very early, the alley looked uninhabited. A dry wind, a pressure change in the atmosphere, made itself felt on my eardrums, and I suddenly found myself in a taxi on the way to the airport. Since the taxi's motion didn't depend on me, I could relax expectantly, delighted that in just a few hours I would be off on a trip. I was just thinking that airplanes weren't dangerous when the taxi stopped at a crossroads. I saw a building in the middle of the fog. The driver turned and we went into the parking lot.

"I'm sorry, but everything is organized so that the customer pays. I know it's expensive," he said as he told me the fee.

I paid and got out.

"I'm sure that I told you the airport. This is the bus station!" I yelled at the driver and got back into the taxi. A funeral procession of cars headed by a hearse passed in front of us.

"Did you know her?" the driver asked.

"Yes," I answered. "It was a neighbor lady. She died last night. She took barbiturates."

VIII

After a leg is amputated the patient believes that his whole body has survived. Nevertheless, when I was separated from my camera I felt that a part of myself had fallen off. I walked toward the hills that surrounded the casino ruins. But, bothered by the feeling that I had forgotten something, that I had forgotten to shave or to shower, I turned around and hurriedly went back, picked up my camera, and hung it around my neck once more. I could make out the entrance to the gardens from far away. I didn't hurry forward. My pulse speeded up and I slowed down; I attempted a gradual approach to the shapeless shell of the casino standing out between the pirul and palm trees. People of all ages congregated around the main garden's railing.

It was one of the first Sundays of the year. All the scenes that had been uninterruptedly taking shape before my eyes came to life in moving strips or balloons of color. With a certain tranquil orderliness, the women's skirts, the men's and boys' plaid shirts all lined up in my furtive glances. Without paying too much attention to myself, and forcing myself not to think about my own problems any longer, I disintegrated in the sudden and uncomfortable feeling of being out of place. The breakfasts in the park and the ball games on the lawn were all parts of my world of more than twenty years ago; that tall grass and those gardens laid out like a series of mazes reproduced in a general sense the old childhood space that I now profaned undeservedly. Perhaps my undirected footsteps, my talent for preventing people from realizing I had them under observation—the expressionless face opposing the backs of women's bodies—allowed me to walk around without anyone paying attention to me, emerging through pathways that upon my passage surrounded me with screaming voices, happy faces, because I looked no different from anyone else except that I wandered around alone. No one follows those of us who wander alone; we pass, and in some way we are invisible.

Before I submerged myself in the weak profundity of the ex-casino, I put a new roll of film in the camera and threw more rolls of film into my pockets. At the same time I fixed my gaze on the colors, the women's faces, the dresses issuing forth from the drawings in the pages of magazines found in the newspaper stands and now superimposed upon female thighs. I picked up a magazine and studied its content page by page, fascinated, as if complete absorption would offer access to its distant and unknown world full of mysteries and prohibitions. Then I saw myself again in the maid's room of my house flipping through fashion magazines. I gave my fullest attention to long hairstyles and the various types of makeup. During one of those summers, which for me took place outside the city, near the beach, I discovered several issues of crumpled magazines in the bushes. The magazines, filled with innumerable sepia photographs and brief captions, offered drawings and images of sculptures. One woman, seen through the crack in a door, whipped another. In a religious ceremony that looked African the eldest woman of the tribe turned around holding a horn between her legs while young women and girls followed her in a trance. The reproduction of a Renaissance oil painting depicted a woman with her hair up and a serene gaze touching her sister's nipple with her fingertips. Sometimes the magazines fell into my hands stripped of covers and titles. I began to peek into dark bedrooms: disguises, smiles aimed at me from inert faces. They accompanied me. I received from those images my fearful initiation, a role model, a set of instructions that oriented me in life without having to expose myself to risk. From then on I was able to name the lipstick traces or wastes that gave away this or that woman in the bus or on the street. A certain excess of color edging the lips defined my father's girlfriend precisely, and I knew all about this woman who ruled over the sulfur-water baths. When I suspected that an inappropriate magazine had fallen into my hands, I immediately felt compelled to look around behind me to make sure there were no potential voyeurs. I returned the magazine to the spot where I found it and continued on my way toward the casino gardens.

On top of the promontory rose the smooth and concave walls of the Agua Caliente tower. I entered at one corner and in the darkness began to climb the metal interior stairwell that spiraled upward. Suddenly, from the first windows of the bell tower, I was able to see the sidewalks below and the traffic, the pedestrians' lightweight clothes, and the heat rising off the streets. It looked as if something was burning nearby because of the way the wind and the sun slapped against people's faces. The damp bell tower room in no way helped mitigate the torpor of the hot, sultry weather. Staring outward—distracted by the people and by the twisted trees below me—seemed to dilute in me that uncomfortable feeling that came over me when I studied a magazine full of nude women. I came to accept, without any pleasure, the apparent certainty that I would live only through my eyes. I had already lost or revised any sense of spatial profundity. I believe I also felt that the sound originating from a portable radio only propagated itself in a fixed direction, and that narrow and sticky wave shoved itself into my head and invaded my whole body; it was as if in that manner I was able to recuperate the sense of volume that sounds always had for me.

I continued upward on one of the wooden ladders that lead from all four sides of the bell tower toward the little tower attic. It was the carpeted, lordly chamber, the palace's most intimate and distant refuge. Beverly and I shared its highest and most tenuously lighted peak, far above the entire landscape of the ruined casino and its devastated gardens. The sun invaded through the cracks growing around the stumpy pilings and in the rooftop shingles. And Beverly remained before me, below me, lying down. Once or twice we tried to come together, but the penetration didn't work. She rose brusquely and told me no, that he would get angry, that it wasn't right, that it was an unforgivable disloyalty. She got down from the bed, her back to me, and began to put on her underwear and her stockings. But very suddenly, in the same capricious and abrupt way, she turned back to me and we fell together onto the bed. And then she was above me, on her knees, and I took into my hand—barely touching it— the sparsely covered, damp, mushroom-shaped head of a baby that came out of her sex, aiming at me . . . The air and the sun spilling over the casino reminded me of other interests. It really was very nice to walk around among the people, to see the children's faces, to pause to drink a soda.

Public gardens usually consist of paths and curves, uncared-for plants and bushes, crossroads, greenhouses that hide the exits. One walks around following whichever objects catch the eye and one gets lost. In the very center of the park, bird cages hang from the trees. Cardinals and parrots from Oceania pose arrogantly and immutably for their admirers. In one corner, several twelve- or thirteen-year-old girls lined up with an older girl who was milking a cow, and she permitted them to try it as well. One by one the young girls went over to touch the cow's udder and they smiled seriously to see the milk squirt out. Various contemplative or happy faces of passersby were swallowed up by my camera's stomach, which was pretending to shoot in other directions. From the second roll of film, which I would be using later, there would emerge numerous pairs of legs and very short skirts. Other little girls stretched out their hands over the seals' pool, reflecting themselves back. The seals played.

One of them swam face up. I climbed on a bench and from that vantage point aimed my camera at that species of female sea lions screaming like newborn puppies. They spent hours and hours stretched out in a sun that warmed them, although it only irradiated them slightly, perhaps because they were wrapped in a layer of fat lying between their skin and their muscles. They had tiny ears with only a barely tangible triangular protrusion. Their little heads stemmed from an imperceptible or nonexistent neck, while their feet divided into fingers and toes that were completely mobile and only slightly hampered by a swimming membrane attaching them. The tail: atrophied to the point of being little more than a stump. The coloration: brown or greenish grey, with reddish or yellowish patches. The skin: lustrous, strong, thick, covered with piglike hairs. I knew that they used their teeth not only to chew but also to hold down and hold onto things. The calves' fur was different from that of the adult seals: they were covered with a thick, delicate white blanket that allowed them to float. Their bodies slipped along as they swam, cylindrical in front and narrowing toward the back. They splashed. They moved with effort, shoving themselves along with their back fins and front feet, like spasmodic jumps. Almost all species of seals achieve the average height of a man or woman. In order to walk they get up slowly and gradually, as if they were inflated with blood, first on their forefeet, dragging their bodies forward in jerks, and then drawing all their extremities together and throwing themselves onto their breasts so as to curve the spine and propel their hindquarters forward. It is a painful advance, but not so much so as to incapacitate them or to annul their heavy slippage that even assumed, at times, a certain pleasurable agility. One of them was dying and it foundered. The rest, captive, seemed to calm down little by little for the spectators, losing their natural shyness. Lazily, a brown seal gulped down the fish that it caught in the air; it splashed around playfully and emerged once more to exhibit itself and be admired. Staring fixedly at them and their games, I saw that they had nothing to do so far from the sea, that this was not the right place for them, but rather their correct space was the dividing line that begins and ends on the beaches. Halfway beings: metamorphosed borderliners; halfway toward life on land; laughing inhabitants of the waves; floating dolls; sleepy, mute, androgynous, and seemingly asexual beings. The seals reappeared and disappeared under the crystalline waters.

Behind the pool a little girl with shorts popped up suddenly next to a statue and then she leaned back against the pedestal. The cast iron figure's body was enveloped in a majestic billowing cape that made the statue seem gigantic and solid, dark and diabolical. I took a picture of the statue and the little girl . . . She was no more than twelve years old; she stared at the camera constantly. We walked alongside each other for a minute or so, and then she ran off to join a group of women and children.

From one of the benches I began to see the small crowd relaxing in the gardens. The idlers that gradually formed groups at the exits made a grey and compact mass. When I focused the camera in their direction I could make out the figure of a little girl walking and turning her head toward me now and again; she was very serious, very sad, very important. The clothing's colors took on a motion of their own. Thanks to that fact I was able to frame the most attractive beings, to capture the parts of their bodies most in accordance with my visual needs.

Beverly was waiting for me in a spot just outside the gardens. It was a grove shadowed by pirul and palm trees, the same place that, years ago, when we were students, hid us from everything and protected us from ill-intentioned gazes. And there were the same branches, the same peppery smell, and the same leaf-covered ground spotted with ripe dates. Beverly stretched out on the grass like a reclining statue; she lifted her hand to her forehead to protect her eyes from the sun. She didn't speak. We began to stroll beneath the bird cages and at that very moment a cardinal escaped through an open door, shooting itself outward, but then, for one second, remaining paralyzed in flight; it couldn't fly any farther and fell vertically against the grass. Beverly watched the last gasps of the red bird flapping at her feet; she picked it up without a word: it was dead. Later, she balanced it in the shell of her cupped hands and placed it gently at the foot of a palm tree. While Beverly distanced herself slowly and mutely through the gardens, I picked up the still-warm dead bird and put it back into its cage and then covered the door with a damp towel. I was left alone among the cages. Beverly returned to the refuge of her bungalow on the beach and soon I imagined her there, I remembered her as she had been the night before, relaxed on the bed, displaying her vaginal lips. Next to her on a night table on the other side of the bed one could see all the instruments necessary to perform an abortion.

"Go to the corner and buy an ice-cream cone."

Then we strolled around. The places we knew together are still there. Nothing has changed. From time to time the buzz of propellers reminds me of the Piper Comanche in which she arrived, but except for those sounds the days pass as a prolongation of her first absences. I hope that someday you will come back to see these places again, this part of the city deformed by highways and still in some manner linked to the splendor of a faded period that barely reveals itself in the cracked walls of the bungalows and the hotels in the process of demolition. I live in one of the houses embedded in the hilltops, in exactly the elevated portion of the hill where the cemetery ends and a new highway toward the sea enters. From here one can see the border, the lights of San Diego Bay, and the police helicopter patrols. The area resembles the south of Italy that is parallel to the Mediterranean Sea. Vineyards and olive and peach trees grow alongside the highway. There are mustard flowers, and at some times of the day the Coronado Islands are outlined sharply against the sea. Thin, worn faces gather at nightfall, return to the beach, and continue on their way. The rest of the peninsula toward the south is arid and mountainous.

It is not at all unlikely that by this time Beverly has reinaugurated her Piper Comanche flights. Probably she gets along by going back to her old habits. By now she will have passed her examination on the first stage of take-off and will have exceeded the required number of hours to qualify her to fly solo. For some time the lessons involved taking off and landing in such quick succession that the tires hardly left the runway for more than a few seconds. The plane barely brushed the surface for a maximum distance of twenty meters, tops, and then took off again. Whenever a small plane crosses the sky, it's possible that there in the pilot's cabin Beverly is in control of the machine.

A Piper Comanche takes off toward the sea and upon crossing the coastal profile turns around and crosses back over the coastline at a low altitude. The nature of the terrain is wild and torn. Dry winds powder the outskirts of the city. The vegetation is nonexistent. Beverly can take that airplane, can cross the reddish mountains of the desert and appear at the top of the valley flying over that city deeply immersed in its crater. Passively rather than with difficulty, the plane allows the wind to carry it, and it seems to float. Before the fringes of the salt flats come into view, the earth changes color; from a greyish brown sprouts the peak of another dry mountain and, gradually, the definitive line between earth and sea. Successive different shades occur in a range of no more than fifty kilometers. In just one region of the valley one could list various geographical possibilities: the lead-colored stone of the embankments, the greenish yellow of the thickets, the stripes of curving asphalt connecting one town to another, the blue sky and the blue sea. The city stretches out toward the hills that create the valley's cradle. Wooden houses constructed with wartime scrap, red roofs, water tanks, weak and recently planted trees—all this turns into tiny spots staining the foothills of the mountains. A mountain sliced open like a loaf of bread emerges from the empty land between the city and the coast; the freeway cuts its way downward and to the sides. High above, backhoes and bulldozers busily bury the remnants of a cemetery without descendants. Above all these items, on the margin of each of these sights, the last lights of the sleeping city begin to vanish. Soon night falls. Propellers begin to spin; engines fit into the thickness of the clouds, and the pilot ambushes the terrorized ants that swarm all over everything. Beverly flies over a black mesa, between canyons and cliffs that, little by little, offer her tranquilizing holes, glimpses of life here and there.

And the B-29, the plane that dropped the first atomic bomb on the city of Hiroshima in 1945, was better known by its crew as the "Enola Gay." It received this name from its flight captain, Colonel Tibbets, from Glidden, Iowa, whose mother's maiden name was Enola Gay Haggard. When Tibbets decided to become a pilot, his whole family objected, with the single exception of his mother, who encouraged him to follow his dreams. The four-ton bomb was baptized with the name "Little Boy." Forebee located the target through his scope at 8 hours, 13 minutes, and 30 seconds. Like a responsible bombardier, he had his finger resting on the manual eject button, in case the synchronization system were to fail. A little earlier, while his assistant, Jeppson, held the flashlight and passed him tools, Parsons had inspected the bomb tube, using extreme care to arm the detonators in the tail of Little Boy with the explosive charge and to secure the contacts to ready the double connection. At that same time, Jake Baser was deeply asleep. When it came right down to it, Forebee didn't need to push the eject button: at 8 hours, 15 minutes, 17 seconds the doors of the bomb bay opened and the mechanism began to sink in the air—like a perfect and majestically extended diver. At 8 hours and 16 minutes the explosion took place.

IX

All at once everything was interrupted. The year hung suspended between June and September. Like a purple parenthesis, the summer, enclosed between two half moons, cuttingly canceled routine and the barrio landscape, the sight of the airport on the hill, the switchman's cottage, the remote and invisible train of every sleepy nighttime. In those days the reservoir had dried up. The city faucets dribbled milky, contaminated water. But we usually left town during the hottest days of August. We spent our vacations in Navojoa and Huatabampo. We left the house empty, in my father's hands. We only heard about the war through adult conversations, when they talked about Squadron 201, about the atomic bomb. In the area around Navojoa, fumigating planes dusted the cotton fields. Day and night the field-workers picked balls of cotton and gathered them up in long canvas sacks. We slept in the open air, on cots, under the stars. We went to the outdoor movies, walked in the plaza, and during the afternoons, on our cots and under a sheet we learned about silence and the lethargy imposed by the valley's oven.

The last days of August scurried away with the same meekness as they arrived, without our even recognizing the drawn-out change of seasons. Suddenly it was over, from one moment to the next. And we packed again for our return to Tijuana. Each time we went, the trip from the desert to the coast took less time. Since there was no paved road, no trains, the long-nosed buses (there were also squashed-nose ones) offered service with all its implicit risks in order to earn the right to that route once conditions improved. No headlights of any other vehicles shone either before or behind us. We penetrated the darkness. The bus driver all at once became too tired to go on and dropped his head on the steering wheel. A passenger volunteered to take his place. I slept with my head on my mother's lap, or sometimes I lay, scared to death, on the pillow created by the sandwiching of my mother and my little sister. At that age I had an impression, my first, very concrete impression of immensity. We chased the opening through the desert; it lost itself curving among the evergreens; we had to follow it through the heat and through the sun that, nearly dissolving, bedded itself in the distance before us. Later on, for hours and hours, my eyes tried to capture the amber glow of the headlights that preceded us, recognizing the road. The yellow spot was the only trace of life between the slippery opening in the desert and my sleeping mother at my side. The man at the wheel lit one cigarette after another and tried to carry on a conversation with the women sitting behind him. After midnight the passengers fell asleep and the silent driver concentrated on the road . . . and on things that I, at that age, was unable to guess.

The night in all its splendor and silence, the open and starry sky—these things lulled me into a soft meditative state, like a daydream, that on the one hand left behind me the placidity of the warm, clean, sunny house of my grandparents in Navojoa, and on the other hand set before me the enigma of a return to an abandoned and unplanned neighborhood, the certain appearance of my father in the bus station where he would be waiting for me with a pack of gum. I remembered him, nevertheless, in his moments of exaltation and talkativeness: his unexpected intrusion into the house as we all slept, the violent brightness of all the lights coming on, his ramblings, his unstoppable monologues imposed upon us in shouts and tense pauses, his forced invitation to have a cup of coffee.

The orange desert sunrise made all these impressions very tenuous. The half-sleep sweetly interrupted by the straight road and infrequent curves, the pleasant passivity of feeling myself transported and the sensation of insufficient sleep: these things added up to the passage between night and day, to the recuperation of my home, to warm milk and games with my sisters, and to the fallen pirul tree in the crevice where we used to hide, but at the same time they foretold of an inevitable, although potentially momentary, hell that I was unable to explain. I felt that I was lying down in the world.

Sedated by the effect of light on the window, by the

quiet of the cacti and of nodding heads, I shook myself awake and focused on contemplating the immediate
future, to corroborate that everything was still as I had
left it.

The red bus stopped on the sharp curves, backed up
and then went forward again, avoiding the Rumorosa
precipices. When I woke, the straight, flat road signaled
summer's end: the cotton fields, the crop-dusting planes,
the recognition of our neighborhood, the new friend-
ships, the dusty bicycle in one corner. Some majestic
white rocks looked newly sprinkled over the landscape,
separated from each other by the volcanic vomit of the
mountains that faded away in the dark and purple distance of the horizon. In the Tecate striations, to one side
of Matanuco's vineyards and interminable olive groves,
terrain was becoming green in some sections barely
brushed by a miserly rain. And the dam's concrete curtain
marked—although I was perhaps the only person on the
bus to recognize it was so—the identical point of departure and of arrival, of abandonment and of reintegration,
a detachment that was never definitive and could always
be postponed.

Underneath the black olive trees olives rotted. I asked
after Beverly and got no response other than silence and
serious faces. I pedaled over to her house, following a
shortcut in the road. I left my bike in the backyard. Someone stuck a box of chocolates in my hand so that I
wouldn't have to go into the house empty-handed. Standing there, absorbed in thought without speaking, it occurred to me that Beverly might have disintegrated. I
went downstairs and saw the remnants of a big party: a
tablecloth and a plethora of plates, cakes, and a kind of
big silver tray upon which, like a golden turkey, lay Beverly with an owllike face, torn apart and mutilated, one

gelatinous eye hanging by a thread. And her whole body looked burned, her arms and legs were broken and stuck out like chicken feet. Next to her, a child on his knees came closer, trying to hold her down, or to console her, or to protect her, and he venerated her, he adored her, and she stared at him. I saw her eyes, I saw that within her eyes she held a painful expression, a maddeningly painful and agonized expression, the gaze of someone who suffers irremediably, who knows there is no salvation for her. I asked myself, Why is she alive? Why don't they kill her?

She looked like a roasted turkey.

X

I wander around linked to my camera. I feel it is an instrument for relating. It seems that I can no longer go on seeing anyone, any woman, with the sole, useless resource of my poor eyes. My naked gaze is of no use to me. I see without seeing, I see without accepting the object's life, without taking into account people's incessant palpitation, without awarding value to that life passing by on the street, marginalized from me, in which I have not been able to take part. The little girl in the shorts felt recognized, she felt she had a place in the world. I pictured her as part of a group, without even noticing that she, individually, vibrated in the middle of the composition at the seals' pool among the other children, the pathways, the statue . . . She stood out, she distanced herself, little by little, from that part of the garden and that group of women, she came up to me and began to walk at my side and snatch little glances at me from out of the corner of her eye. I know that she was looking at me, and I see myself in profile next to her. The replacement telephoto lens, when added to the camera, is long and cylindrical and sticks out upright in front. As soon as the little girl changed direction and entered into focus as she distanced herself from me, I shot. I shot several times. Many times. I kept shooting until I ran out of film and out of breath, until the mechanism that moves the film forward broke down.

I didn't have any other way of looking except through the telephoto lens. I searched out a couple and calculated the shot; I waited for the instant in which they were perfectly framed as I walked along, and when I realized the couple was turning their backs on me, I reacted instinctively and I shot them. That kind of perfect moment often coincided with music coming from some radio, and that inopportune intrusion was enough to make me react instinctively and press down the shutter as if I could photograph sound. Capture it. Hold it. Paralyze it in the same way that I anxiously froze images.

The darkroom smelled like lemon, and that's where I collected all the used camera cartridges. For months all I did was store them away. I only entered the room to photograph myself, as I did every day in front of the easel, and to refill the camera. I went out into the street, attentive to the imaginary angles formed from above by the bridge where the train passed every night. Down below, the Agua Caliente houses were unable to hide their red roofs in the pirul trees. It was like a Sunday in a school playground. It was surrounded by silent, sad frames.

The casino's bungalows, the wooden sidewalks, the tennis courts were all empty. There was no one on the neighboring beach and no sign of life near the sulfur baths. There was just one person, a small skinny kid, bouncing a ball on the basketball court behind the fence. A study in black and white: the player moved back and forth in front of me without ever heading toward the sidelines, his image was a grey-toned splotch despite his red-and-white Pegasus sweatshirt. The player tried out a number of shots, jumped, ran, dribbled the ball against the clay court; he lifted himself up onto his toes and for the fraction of a second he was in the air, in that precise and unpremeditated second, the result of a perfectly studied movement, he tossed the ball toward the net. He grew upward for a few seconds and threw the ball toward the basket with all the force in his little, stiff, strong body. The backboard vibrated, wobbling back and forth a little and squealing. I didn't shoot the picture insolently. No. I leaned back on a bench and soon saw myself inside four fences, like the inside of a cage echoing with the distant sound of the ball hitting the ground.

During the whole time I was sitting there I never realized that the basketball player (who must have been between twelve and fifteen years old and was wearing white tennis shoes and red Pegasus shorts) had on a kind of golf cap, one of those woolen Irish affairs, sewn together in sections, that were modeled in Chaplin movies; but no, it wasn't, now that I come to think of it, it was very clearly a jockey's cap. For a second, and without any apparent connection, it reminded me of the pictures that I had taken of Beverly (when she was getting dressed in the hotel room and I told her wait a minute, sit down in this chair, and let me take a picture of you) and that with the passage of time lost their color stored away in that absurd archive of letters and useless objects. I remained seated, watching the solitary basketball player who kept dribbling the ball indefatigably. I crossed my legs and right there in front of me, at fifty meters, more or less, from the camera's sight, the tiny, slim figure of the jockey kept right on playing, and his figure slowly, bit by bit, began to define itself in the viewfinder until I was able to see it

clearly. The more or less distant silhouette became
sharply cut out and gradually centered itself in the frame
I had chosen: the basketball player, or golf player, or
jockey, or dwarf, was ready to be trapped definitively, to
be etched into celluloid before anyone could prevent it
from happening. The ball flew through the air. The
player, showing off the sweatshirt with the embroidered
letters spelling out Pegasus, leaped up to capture it. The
rebound was perfect. The eaglelike leap impeccable. He
threw from behind his back, without touching the hoop.
Rebounded. From the white line, in the most distant corner of the court. Dribbled between his legs. The ball spun
on a fingertip. The jockey ran toward the camera's center;
he came, he went, he spun, made a long jump like the
track athlete's triple jump and spotted, slam dunked, lay
the ball inside the basket. Free throws. Half-court shots.
The camera stopped working. I put it back against my
chest. I returned the shutter to its resting position, like
someone putting the safety on a gun, and put the camera
away in its leather holster. Then, one by one, I jumped
over the Agua Caliente tower's bells, which had been set
out on the grass after the fire that destroyed the casino's
traditional entrances.

The tower had four Mozarabic arches at its base and
was memorable for combining a Turkish mosque style of
architecture with a vague decomposition of a hybrid Californian style, which made the tower look vaguely colo-
nial and vaguely Andalucían at the same time. In the casino years, caravans of automobiles entered the grounds
by passing under the tower arches; later on, school buses
and teachers' cars filled the old structure on a daily basis.
The tower also served as a symbol to the students who,
day after day, crossed under its four oval gateways in or-

der to go to class. Cherry-colored student sweaters frequently covered the ruins of the tower that, years earlier,
when the other side of the border suffered under the dry
laws, had been erected over a fragile wooden scaffolding
reinforced with chicken wire and stucco. Numerous fragments from the tower's interior, especially the bells, were
covered with chalk. Students' names, dates, young couples who had recently fallen in love, memories, and nick-
names had been secretly recorded, and they provided a
ciphered communication for those kids who, during class
time, snuck around to hide themselves on the stairways
in the tower's stomach in that halfway sunken neighborhood where a school had been dumped into the walls of
the old Agua Caliente casino so that they could smoke
and talk and laugh and get bored and sleep and tell stories
and tell good and bad gossip about people and wish they
had Marta, Celia, Elisa in there with them until the classes ended and night closed over the sky and the teachers
and the buses would disappear forever into the peripheries of town.

   The only way to tell the casino and the center of scholarship apart was by the clothes and the behavior of the
new inhabitants. Before and a little after 1930, the motion
was different. The rhythm of visitors went up on the
weekends, especially during the summer. Tourists came
from La Jolla, Santa Monica, San Bernardino, or San
Juan Capistrano and they spent the day at the beach or
in the pools. They protected their skin in the shade of the
palm trees imported from Hawaii that lined all the casino
walkways; and later on they took over the night in its
most ardent phases. Black and cream-colored luxury cars
entered the casino through the tower arches after detach-
ing themselves from the international border, or drove

swiftly down the boulevard after picking up their air taxi clients at the airport. After passing under the tower archway, the cars drove down a slope next to the palm tree–lined avenues. Elegant women stepped down from Packards and DeSotos in the doorway of the Salón de Oro; they paused for a moment in the vestibule while the chauffeur drove off with the car and someone came out, if they were not accompanied, to escort them into the ballroom. In those days my father used to wear a corduroy suit and white shoes set off with a contrasting bit of black leather. He was one of the telegraph operators employed in the casino hippodrome to take long-distance bets from the fans in California. Couples entered and left the hotels and the bungalows. Later on, it was almost impossible to hear traffic sounds in the silence of the countryside and the screaming of the gambling rooms. An aged doorman with cottonlike hair waited in the doorway of the Salón de Oro's mosaic patio to bid farewell to the gamblers and their ladies at dawn. There's a picture from those years, and in it my father is surrounded by a group of friends at the foot of a trimotor airplane whose wing seemed to embrace them all. When my father rubbed his nose, you could see a wound on his upper lip that later on would be covered by a reddish mustache. On Saturdays a large percentage of California's population came to empty itself into the city. I saw late-model cars on the boulevard. Mondays were different; the city looked so unpopulated that it seemed as if it had been the object of a mass evacuation. The sulfur baths and the golf courses looked desolate. Nevertheless, this Friday to Sunday floating process of overpopulation continued to recur as the city's normal mode of existence even when President Lázaro Cárdenas closed down the casino and turned it into a school.

XI

My lips tremble.

You were always the same woman with different names—the neighborhood girl, the middle-school classmate, the recently married woman, the casino prostitute—or the same woman, you yourself, when you allowed yourself to be pursued at a certain distance through the airport sidewalks minutes after I saw you descend from the yellow airplane. At the same time, I could imagine, despite all the confusion from which I am unable to escape and that will inevitably prevent my spontaneity, that in some way you have had something to do with all the women locked up in the sulfur bathhouses, that you reigned in that world and didn't allow anyone to escape, even though you figured among those women individually and despite the fact that you, at least, are no longer around to listen to me. I don't discount that you still remain in this quiet body and in my very own face contemplated in the mirror, because I have lived with myself since I was born and even now I have not been able to get outside of myself completely. But I knew perfectly well and with a terrifying clarity that I began to love you the day that you left. I tried to search for you throughout the whole world. In my dreams I would hug a cat for days, weeks, after watching you leave. How odd, I would tell myself; I am falling apart again. Or, how wonderful, I need you again, I need to see you come by yourself to the school's nighttime halls and to muss your hair, and feel once again the joy of strolling down streets and more streets and the inexhaustible habit of stopping in the Spanish restaurant to drink beer from the same mug. All the scarcity, Beverly. All that you never had. They didn't teach you to notice, they didn't tell you that you also had a right to everything, to leave your hometown if you wanted to; no one close to you ever told you that there was nothing wrong with that. No one was there to listen to you and to understand that what you said was true for you. You looked at yourself in the mirror, you touched your facial bones, felt the incipient wrinkles in your eyelids. It was the first time that you were alone with yourself but you were not absolutely sure and you saw in the mirror that you had grown up. I try to define you and I fail. I try to make sense of you, to examine you, and I overflow with words, just exactly the same as when I tried to write you so many failed letters. I wanted to speak to you as if you existed or as if I wasn't addressing myself to you, because overnight, one long-ago day, I realized I was talking to myself, referring to you in the third person, and I was even talking to myself out loud as I strolled down the beach among the flotsam of that place and that what I have lived with you had transformed me and torn me to bits. I told myself that, bit by bit, as time went on, I would be able to pull together the pieces of my dispersed self and reintegrate them so that I could heal myself, understand myself, and grow up. I have been very fearful of death; I thought about you, but after a while I began to understand that the only death I really cared about was my own. You escape me, you leave me, and I vainly attempt to bring you back to me once again, I try to modify you or invent you at any point in the world or in the past. Once again we will eat smoked fish on that beach; I would imagine you all alone and I could foretell each and every thing that you would do there, far away, alone, each morning, each afternoon, during the slow passage of the day, and I would locate you in your sadness and depression perhaps because only in that way would I be able to recognize you from my point of view. Or I would give

another twist to my delirium and I would tell myself that
no, you would never allow yourself to become sad, just
because, for no other reason than that you shouldn't be,
it's no good and meanwhile, for right now, at least you're
alive. In other words, I would invent you. I would manage
to make you an irreconcilable enemy and in that way to
keep you outside myself, more mine.

"Pass me the sugar . . ."
    "I never should have looked at your letters."
    "They're not important. I never would have done it. I'd
get bored . . ."
    "Forgive me."
    "We barely touch."
    "I suppose you never formed an impression of me."
    "It's likely."
    "I sometimes ask myself if I really knew you."
    "I used to like to walk barefoot in the sand. The dunes,
I said. I had never heard that word before . . . The ovens
for smoking fish, the eucalyptus leaves, the smoke . . ."
    "Now we belong to each other so little, perhaps not at
all. Then . . . I remember the dryness of your lips."
    "I don't understand this delayed reaction."
    "I lived through several blank months. I entertained
myself with absurd trips . . . It was like a generalized inability to feel. But, obviously, one can't live in ecstasy forever, that's not what I'm talking about. You just don't figure it out so quickly. I haven't figured it out yet."
    "Probably I didn't know how to see you. And I swore
that I would never be unfeeling about any requests . . ."
    "It's very likely that even now I am not able to express
myself . . . And later on, to disturb the life you made for
yourself, when you had already left behind you a long and
truncated experience that held no value whatsoever . . . It

seemed obligatory that I not call you, not see you. Like the least I could do. But I couldn't avoid it."

"It will never seem like a dream to me."

"I didn't know if my hand was your hand, if you were the one moving or if it was me. I didn't know if it was you or I who thought of something."

"We were a monster, then."

"Yes, a single body."

"If it were not for the fact that I lay on your chest and heard your heartbeats . . ."

"We licked from the same ice-cream cone."

"So inexpressive, never saying anything."

"But, why does everything have to be formulated in words?"

"I don't know. You go someplace where people are gambling with their lives and the only thing you think about is your freedom, which is always false anyway. It worries you. You imagine that it might be important."

"What I am telling you is that I can't say anything. Whether they like me or not . . ."

"But that has nothing to do with it."

"No, you just wouldn't understand."

"At least don't be so lazy. I'm just saying."

"You also love sleeping."

XII

The casino walls were all a meter thick. It was the typical kind of prewar construction: high, thick masonry walls covered with stucco and then whitewashed. Brick-colored roof tiles overlapped the bungalows like visors and covered the walls that enclosed the thermal springs on the other side of the bridge over which the train passed, whistling, every night.

Right where the embankment interrupted the gravel, a pathway detached itself to lead toward the baths, those springs of high-temperature holy water, the medicinal water, the baths with no Virgin of Lourdes. Beyond those walls that hid foreign nudists, several women emerged from the concrete compartments dividing the pool and went into the huts next door. Beer and soda advertisements and engraved signs plastered the doorways to the thermal baths. Several roads merged there, outside the baths and a few steps away from the riverside cabarets. Between classes at the Agua Caliente Institute we watched yellow taxis and uniformed sailors arrive with the beginning of summer. We could make out the women awaiting them: tiny, distant figures, young women and old women just coming out of the water, still drying their hair, hairbrushes in their hands, smelling of ordinary soap. Some were fat, some wore pants, some wore slips; the women stretched lazily and breathed deeply, sensuously, as they stepped down from the beds or emerged naked from their first swim in the sulfur waters. The panorama was less open at nighttime. Then it was hard to see even the taillights of the taxis as they drove toward the bathhouses, marked by small and intermittently shining red lights.

But where or who could I ask about Beverly, since the last time she came to this part of the city all there was left of the casino was rubble, and the springs had all dried up? What use was the sea's proximity to me, what sense did it make to sit stupidly contemplating the bungalow where she had spent some days, a few nights, alone with me, totally divorced from that distant world to which she returned?

It was of no use. A string of prefabricated walls and the reflection of neon lights hit my eyes: Blue Fox, Aloha,

Waikiki. I parked the car on the tennis court. I took several rolls of film out of the trunk of the car and distributed them in my pockets. I took the camera out of its case and hung it around my neck. I put it next to my heart as if preparing for a second possibility for sight, another eyehole, another resource, an additional optical apparatus that would assist me in capturing and fixing forever those ruined buildings that I couldn't stop to explore because of the suspicious gaze of the military police officer stationed there in the school, there in the ex-casino, there in the guardhouse behind the palm tree. I paused before the Arabic portal of the Salón de Oro. I saw my face in the water. A damp, shapeless spar was half-sunk under its depths; scraps of paper and rotten flowers floated on the muddy surface without managing to obstruct the sparkle of the filigreed horses' heads barely attached to the fountain's rusted arch. Grass nearly covered the time-worn pavement. The enormous tile-decorated Cinderella doorway soon gave way to another huge door, this one with broken windows and boards nailed across it, barring it shut. A chain prevented entry. I stuck the camera through a hole in the broken glass and reached one hand out to try to grasp one of the posters attached to the faded mosaic, one that was beginning to fall off under some burnt struts. On the poster I could still vaguely make out the picture of Rita Cansino. All there was in the background was trash, firefighters' footprints, smashed cigarette packages, beer cans, empty condom envelopes, wet magazines, and bits of crumpled newspaper stained with feces.

The neighboring building had been the hotel and dining room, and it was precisely there, on the doorway lintels, where the words carved by students stood out: the obscene words, the necessary words that everyone had to set down in order to express themselves, anonymous insults about the principal, or declarations of love in carved initials. And over these signs, over these stains, over these sentences, other ways of integrating the syllables fell into place, other ways of putting together sentences, of imposing a capricious typography, of combining capital letters and Gothic or italic type over Roman numerals, scattered formal exercises, drawings, figures, the coordinates of obscene poetry.

Inscrutable tunnels honeycombed the lower levels of the casino. Between classes, or after school when the neighborhood was left abandoned, the tunnels that connected so many different and diverse underground areas were converted into a fascinating labyrinth of solitary games, of persecuted and terrified girls. They were cloisters of laughter and echoing voices; the ghosts of Rita Hayworth and of Jean Harlow's lover. They were home to the adolescent searches for the legendary nymphomaniacs. Green felt tabletops, roulette games, billiard tables, pianos and player pianos, posters half-absorbed into stucco like Renaissance paintings. And it was there where I would find you again. You would be sitting on the grass near the tennis courts. Many years later you would tell me that at that time, when we were about to finish junior high school, you were going to give me the photo from your ID card. We were already in our last year and we would not see each other again after exams. I didn't dare ask you for the photograph or even speak to you. Later that night you sat down, all alone, without seeing me, in the audience gathered in the conference room of the Salón de Oro for the concert that was already taking place. Once more the designs on the walls and the curtains made each of us call to mind *their* world; they carried our attention away to other, distant vistas—to the ceiling's flat sky full of painted women and dresses, to the worn carpet where we followed the broken filigrees—all images that perpetually enacted a gala dinner in a casino dissolved in time.

The dusty cherry velvet curtains that formerly opened and closed before the proscenium had by now fallen into disuse and were kept permanently open. Dusty cherry velvet and the silhouettes of dancers reappeared and disappeared throughout "Rosamunda." The women had just seated themselves at the table in their transparent white gauze dresses and pointed-toe patent-leather shoes. Bubbles rose in glasses of champagne. Crystal goblets of air and water blended with the cigarette holders of the women and the smoke and scattered laughter from the conversations, and waiters rushed by, moving in an orderly fashion from table to table. High starched collars, Rudolph Valentino hairstyles, pouchy eyes heavily made up; the tall, thin, erect waiters jumped attentively, attending to the caprices of the entertaining women standing next to the roulette boards and the one-armed bandits between the dining room and the Salón de Oro, before, during, and after the ball held on sunflower carpets, foamy and red, at the same time as one heard shouts and saw the women's legs in the flat sky of the conference room, on the walls behind Beverly and Beverly's gaze. Her high collar, her canvas bag, her flannel jacket, her wide, almost rhomboidal eyes like those of a woman in a Modigliani painting: because her long, soft neck and the blonde and chestnut hair covering her ears integrated Beverly into the painted groupings and made her stand out from the rest of the concert's audience, distinguished her among the heads and the bodies in the darkened auditorium. And the Récamier chair where you posed like a maja? Make a portrait of me, you said. Silk-covered doors and mirrors hanging on the walls stretched from the floor to the chandeliers. I pressed the camera's shutter a number of times and you emerged from the shadows, dark and distorted as if there was not enough light in the room . . . But you would never see those pictures. Outside the hotel, through the window, one could see a tennis court, grass grown overly long, and a solitary basketball player, the same one whose figure repeated itself in the photographs I developed later. The palm trees didn't show up against the sun; the direct light cast a veil over the film, and one could barely make out the fuzzy outlines of a broken-down palm tree. The control tower of the old airport leaps upward over the casino's shell. It is the tallest part of the ruins; it is crowned with tiles; it's blue and retains its framing battlements and the stairways that rise and fall from the heights of this infantile medieval castle. At the foot of the mosque an old man sweeps garbage into a pile. He looks like a lighthouse guard. He gives orders to the young man that Sunday when you dressed up in a tie, sweater, and woolen pants. He tells the young man to pick up the dry leaves and garbage that fall from the trees, the ripe dates, the palms, and he stares pensively at the little mountain of garbage that is slowly beginning to burn.

In the midst of the silence I sense Beverly's imminent appearance. I believe I see her again in one of the casino tunnels. I search for her, despite the fact that I am certain I will never again have the opportunity to speak to her, and to have her listen to me. I know that she was able to shut me up, that she taught me to be mute. When we met in the airport she told me she had never seen the photos. Don't tell me you never got your set of photographs. For three or four years I've been determined to get rid of the archive, to destroy memory and the past by tearing apart

something material; I have decided not to save anything
related to all that which has now vanished. What no
longer exists is no longer worthwhile. Not a single photo,
you commented. Some people never keep a single letter.
I watched you, finding it odd. Just like now, when I have
totally forgotten you, because you never let me know that
everything that showed up in those images was totally
true and you never helped me to prove that it had been
me, and no one else, who had taken those pictures.
Really, I couldn't get over my astonishment, particularly
after I began, with great pride, to develop your photographs myself, with my own hands, in the darkroom; and
after prolonged and fascinating experiments, after having
purchased matte developing paper of a specific weight, I
brought forth a marvelous pair of pictures of you: in a
boutique in front of a full-length mirror, next to another
couple, and the other in which I captured you against a
wall full of posters. Precisely in the very instant of seeing
you climb down from the plane, I was there with that
waiting face, that unblushing face full of tranquil curiosity, just to hear you speak of something else and without saying anything to you yet about the need to break
up with you, I allowed you to continue talking and I
waited once again for your quick and enthusiastic answer
because I enjoyed working with those photographs so
much. I had watched you emerge from the water bit by
bit. I changed you from one liquid to another, and then I
held you down and I lingered when I began to distinguish
clearly between the blacks and the greys and the whites
on the developing paper. It was as if you were born an
adult, dripping, from out of a generous white shell, from
out of a mythic maritime foam. And I repeated the pro-
cedure with fascination and an almost alchemical hope.
I took you. I looked at you under the red light and finally

I achieved my goal of revealing you in the darkroom where you had been born and where you had surged forth in a few seconds of light and water, and once more, sweepingly aqueous, you lay down to dry. I cut you. I sought out all the diverse angles and frames with the paper cutter. And the next day you appeared stepping down from the yellow airplane: living, palpable, and agreeably warm in my hands. It was then that I kissed you uncontrollably, waiting in silence to hear you tell me that, yes, in fact, you had received the photos and that you adored them, that you thought they were studio photographs. But things didn't happen that way. I had the feeling everything was lost and I realized that to live with no relation to anyone or anything was—provisionally, perhaps—the best choice. Ever since that flight I exiled you from the country forever; I proposed locking myself up in my room and never speaking again, even to myself. I wouldn't let anyone know about your disappearance. Our common friends, if we ever had any, no longer existed for me.

I hope that someday you come back to all these places: to the pathways that run through the patios between decayed groupings of buildings and classrooms, the dormitory basements stuffed full of furniture and boxes, playing cards and green-felt–covered tables, mildewed roulette games, and pianos deprived of keys. I hope. We would no longer be frightened. We would meet each other again in the casino rubble and we would see the birdcages in the gardens. You could go back to the same spot and I would be waiting for you as always. It will have been at least six months since we saw each other. You would wear sunglasses. You would look as if you recently showered, as if you just came out of the sea. You would put your hand on the car window as though you wanted to hold the door shut with your body for as long as the green light allowed you to keep going. The long lines of cars, the sun would all exacerbate my confusion, preventing me from realizing that this could already be the last time I would ever see you. Nevertheless, another possibility for a reencounter could present itself. Some Saturday, in a bar like the Blue Fox, very cold, and then you and he, each on your own side, you watching me without saying a word: we'd see each other later for sure . . .

I'm talking about your last visit to the border. Finally I see you come out of the parking lot where I immediately recognize your car and the California license plates. You look down the street and at the people passing by and you walk along calmly. You put on your sunglasses. It's cloudy, but you look good in them. Your long hair falls to both sides of your un-made-up face. It looks as though you have just arrived from a very long trip. We hug. I lay my cheek against yours nervously, fearful that you might pull yours away abruptly. Months without seeing each other. You have nothing to say to me. Did you tell me that you had been on a leper island? The sulfur-water pool has a slimy, slippery bottom. Dark places, halls, chunks of crystallized salt. Green-black water. You are sitting down. The lepers bathe themselves. Their bluish skin shudders. They don't have any hair; you can see their heads are swollen, and you can see their veins. They go into the water fully dressed. You hesitate. You bathe with them. You walk in water to your waist. You begin to remove your clothes. Someone has told you that they are not contagious . . . What would we do, how would we survive if our bodies were not a constellation of holes: pores, mouth? We'd explode.

He, the cold and distant man who accompanies you at the Blue Fox, ought to be the third character. Your husband, your fantasy lover. The master pilot. The captain. The aviator devoured by the sky. The significant absence in your bungalow by the embankment, your irrecoverable master. You showed me the photograph you had in your wallet in which you are sitting by a fountain next to some trees; you are looking down at your toenails, you are wearing sandals and your face doesn't show up well. In those places, you told me, you can walk barefoot everywhere, even when it rains, because it is so hot and the earth is cool. I loved to listen to you. Where were the lepers? In the casino pool or in the sulfur-water ponds? Water that rests the bones. Water that smoothes the muscles. Water that crushes the cornea. Water where logs float to save the lives of the shipwrecked. Salt water from which female sea lions emerge. Halfway. Half the body. Barely. Awash with water.

You told me that some day I ought to go to Mulegé, that it smells like peaches, like cooked rice, like tangerines, that the mountains howl at night. While I listened to you, I planned to visit those places you talked about, the edges of the salt flats, the towns with Franciscan churches and convents, the interminable green and silver beaches, the hammocks, the many-colored houses, and the seaside terraces.

The dunes, you told me, are shaped like tongues and they form behind any windbreak. It's a place full of the hidden treasures of galleons and miniature brigantine vessels. I would have liked to see you touch the frescoes and the bas-reliefs carved into the walls. I imagined you alone in the small central garden at the heart of the convents, under the archways, leaning against walls with filmy stains. That afternoon, as you stepped down from the car, walked toward me, accepted my hug, strolled along with me, I promised myself not to interrupt you too much. My goal was not preventing the transmission of what I felt deep inside, nor hiding any thoughts that might make me seem cold to you. I looked wherever you looked when you moved your lips. I sketched a drawing in your notebook and I wrote your name several times. You had changed addresses a lot; some phone numbers looked familiar to me. I saw my name and one of my old addresses.

You are inside a telephone booth. You put a coin in the slot; you are wearing sandals and a loose dress. I walk around the phone booth. You lift up one foot. You drop one of the sandals on the floor; you twist yourself up in the cord and the receiver. You laugh; you listen quietly. I don't know who you are talking to. I can't hear what you're saying. Now, whenever I see an empty telephone booth I feel like going inside and closing the door so that I don't die of cold. You used to have a lot to talk about in those days. Another night: you are sitting in a café; you are wearing a blue coat and you drop it when you take it off and then you sit on it. I scratched a decal off the window and peered in at you through the hole; you were smoking while he was telling you about who knows what. I left. I walked around the block, and when I didn't see you in the same place when I got back, I ran home. I wanted to die. I threw things around uncontrollably, I ran outside, enormously upset, and I hurried through streets and more streets without stopping. I stood on a street corner waiting for you to come by. After midnight, buses and cars roared under the underpass and I saw how life went on inside of them apart from me, without my intervening, without my lifting a finger, without my participation. When I saw you again in the casino gardens you told me that you were tired of it all, that you simply did not want to do anything, and you insisted upon that. I have been very lucky, I tried to convince you. But you kept coming back to the same theme. Do something. Get out of here. Go somewhere, make some decisions for good or ill, but do something, for chrissake, go to Cuba, to Africa, you said desperately, although not very convincingly. How profound we were that night, the "typical destructive attitude," our "role in the world," and then there was nothing else I could do but grab your hand by force and push you around to make you react; I slapped your face, your lips, and once again the clichés: "our duty to be happy," that's all, "this relationship is not going anywhere." I stuck you in the car and I drove you to the city morgue. All I had to do was shove against the barrier in order to get the car inside and reach the center of the patio surrounded by buildings, and after crossing through metal doors and cold hallways I closed you in behind the door of the refrigerated room in the back. I heard you screaming for several eternal seconds; you pounded on the door and kicked it. You came out terrorized but calmer, you hugged me sobbing, and you told me that you didn't want to talk about it anymore, and blah blah blah, and that this is the last time, that I need you, that you must never leave me alone. When we got home, after covering you up with the quilts I told you that I would give you a spanking the next time you behaved that way.

XIII

I go outside, and when I realize that I have forgotten my camera, I feel as if a part of my body has been cut off. I stick my nose in a magazine. I stare at the fashion section. I concentrate on a single paragraph as if in that block of writing I could find a corresponding echo, a fact I can identify with; as if my need to belong would be satisfied, my wish for communion discovered there, in a phrase, in the words she quoted, Beverly's words, and Beverly saying that things dilute, speaking of one buried love or another, saying that substitution is always possible. And then I turn back and I walk and I see—materially see— my last two or three years of self-absorption, and I am uncertain if those years at her side were really worth living. I suspect that I detest her, that everything is worthless, that it has been more than two or three years since I've last seen her, and if I reject her it is because those things—for her—really are important. Because she never learned to live alone. Because I have actually been able to construct a world for myself that, in some ways, I have grown accustomed to. Because how can one satisfy oneself with only oneself? How to enclose oneself, be sufficient unto oneself, wallow in one's own naked body before the mirror, smell one's own odors? The lack of sleep, the flesh of my own body, of my own masculine body, observed almost to the point of self-possession. Will this perhaps be the method for strangling the desire that I ought to have every morning when I go outside and gaze at women's legs, women's eyes, women's asses, women's gazes, women's silent and occult messages—all the women: the girls, the married ladies, the divorced women, the abandoned widows, the sisters, the aunts, my mother's girlfriends, friends' wives—that rubbing of myself with my own body and feeling as dirty as the first time I ejaculated? And she still remains vulnerable to some words; it is the relationship that healed, it is her remaining alone and forging ahead. I review the years after her and am painfully aware of a grave sense of waste and everything that signifies waste; I squander myself and the drops that I sprinkle uselessly on the sheets, the act that I exercise alone to alleviate, to cancel my potential, my certain, early-morning desire. I have lost count of the sperm before they accumulate, and later I dream that I am seated on a ravine, or on a decaying bridge in the middle of a lake, or on a bluff overlooking the sea. A fishing pole is in my hand. There is resistance at the end of the line. A body pulls at it beneath the water. The line tangles between my fingers, marks them, cuts my skin. I pull the line, along with the attached object, toward me. A fish emerges flapping from the water face up. I look at it lying at my feet—it's mine, it's rising toward me, it's mine, it's following the line up between my legs, it's mine—and then the fish expires on the sand—it's mine, it flaps, it's mine, it falls still, it's mine, damp and sprinkled with sand.

XIV

In just one moment, from one day to the next, the world changes. Everything falls out of place and becomes strange. It's all the same to me. Sometimes the only things I'm really interested in are eating and sleeping—sleeping a lot and believing that on that night when the plane landed on the beach it was so dark that we were unable to see each other's faces and in that way unable to recognize that we were prisoners of our own panic and doubt. The afternoon that had just faded away absolved us of all guilt and we are waiting for the man with the bag to get out of the plane and for the pilot to hide the airplane to one side of the poorly lit landing strip in an improvised hangar made of chicken wire and canvas.

I go to meet the man who has stepped down from the plane, and we talk in English. The man is wearing a wrinkled black overcoat. I open the bungalow door and direct

him to Beverly's room. I leave them alone. I go out and
walk on the embankment without ever losing sight of the
weak glow of the bungalow lights. I wait for the hours to
go by, and I sit on an abandoned cart. The darkening sea
seems pacified. I know that it is cold; the Alaskan current
icily sweeps down the coast of Baja California. Even by
the lunar light, the sea cannot manage to draw the line
that defines it against the background: a kind of black
wind confuses the sea with the prolongation of the sky.
The tiny lights of a fishing boat displace themselves intermittently toward the south and are lost. I feel the
breeze pick up and advance toward me. The cold and the
realization that over two hours have gone by move me to
get up. I look at the light glowing in Beverly's room. The
man pulls aside the curtain, seeking me in the darkness.
As I come closer to the bungalow I can see that he has
left the front door halfway open; he seems to make a sign
to the airplane pilot like someone calling his chauffeur. I
don't ask him anything. He has the same dry, professional
look on his face as when he arrived; no trace of satisfac-
tion or exhaustion crosses his forehead. The small wrinkles denote a more-or-less bad mood. I give him the
money and immediately go to Beverly's room. Next to
her—sleeping, weakened—there is a pot full of hot water.
I smell alcohol-dampened sheets. I hear the airplane take
off on the beach, its roar, and then the buzzing fades
away, diminishing little by little until it dissolves on the
other side of the Rumorosa mountains. I let Beverly sleep
that night without saying anything to her, sitting next to
her bed. When she wakes up, the room is clean. I've taken
away the pot of freezing water and have thrown the sur-
gical instruments used by the doctor as far as I can onto
the beach. The salty seawater isn't potent enough to get
rid of the strong ammonia smell left on my hands from

handling the dishes and the damp towels. I try to forget my earlier conversations with Beverly; I try to accept that there is no life before the first month, that there is nothing wrong with what we're doing, that it is irresponsible to have a child in our current situation. Beverly sits up carefully and speaks to me. She looks at me. She looks at me but I am not certain that she wants to say anything to me. She is not frightened. I'm the one who has not been able to overcome my fear. I haven't been able to sleep. I was sure that someone was spying on us. In fact, watching the sea and trying to calm my thoughts has been my only resource to try and forget, for a moment, the shadows and the imaginary footsteps that I believed were creeping up behind me. By the time the sun has finally made an appearance, I have Beverly's belongings stored in the car. She is no quieter than usual when I take her by my side. She seems to doze on my shoulder as we come out of the pass and take the region's main highway.

"I'll drive," I tell her. "You sleep."

We drive up the coast the whole length of the new highway. The sea extends before us in a wide blue semicircle. Without going into the city we take the road that runs parallel to the fence at the international border. There are very few cars in line at this time of day. The border guard asks to see our documents, and I show him my multiple-entry visa. He asks for hers. I tell him that she's not feeling well. He insists. I look for Beverly's passport in her purse and suddenly see myself between the impatient officer and the woman propped up on my right shoulder. In that fraction of a second I see her at my side again, and I recall the previous few minutes when I had been driving on the coastal road watching the sea and the beach fall behind us in my rearview mirror. The officer didn't wait for me to articulate my sudden misgivings and insistently de-

manded her passport one more time. I told him she was
sick. He insisted on speaking to her and brusquely shook
her shoulder, but Beverly did not answer. Then I felt
something cold soaking my pants. I squeezed my eyes
shut in an effort to erase the image of a bullfighter with
a wounded thigh that had suddenly appeared in the momentary darkness of my closed eyes. In that way, with my
eyelids shut, I felt my two legs and Beverly's thigh resting
next to mine. The officer's awkward shove on Beverly's
shoulder shook me out of my lack of awareness. Beverly's
body suddenly tipped to the right and the blood was
there, underneath her thighs. On my hands. I didn't touch
anything else. I didn't touch the steering wheel. I remained with my hands out, paralyzed.

"Of course I read the book. I liked it a lot . . . and your
dedication, too: 'So that you learn to disobey.' "
    "Do you still have it?"
    "Yes, I'll keep it forever."
    "We ought to have gone back to the beach. I really liked
the smoked fish, eating it with our fingers . . . "
    "With lemon . . ."
    "Didn't you want to go in?"
    "Afterward I did."
    "I could tell you didn't like it."
    "It wasn't such a big deal."
    "There were two spots in the book. I remember per-
fectly well. A blue one and a yellow one. Little Blue and
Little Yellow. First they played together, and strolled
through the park. Later they merged little by little; they
clasped their hands together and produced one green
spot between them. Then half of their bodies also turned
totally green. Pages later all you could make out was a
single big green spot. A single body."

"But after that the same process happened again, slowly, in reverse . . . And then abruptly. They became half green again. Then barely the tips of their linked hands showed even the tiniest speck of green, and then they released their hands . . ."

"And the blue spot and the yellow spot separated, and each went off on its own. Little Blue and Little Yellow."

"A children's story . . ."

XV

I was behind bars. There were several interrogations. Someone wanted to accuse us of dealing with clandestine hospitals or with a clinic on wheels, towed behind a car, that picked up its clients along the highway. They tried to connect us with a ranch house that had also been identified. They subjected me to confrontations with unknown people, foreign and Mexican doctors. I saw trembling hands and faces, greedy eyes, judicial offices. A bulletproof vest hung from a coatrack. A display window ostentatiously showed off lines of rifles and machine guns. Apparently someone had claimed Beverly's body and taken it to San Francisco.

They couldn't connect me with any criminals and I repeated that we had made arrangements through anonymous contacts, that it took place in an improvised clinic whose location and description I didn't remember, and that we gave false names. They took away my belt and my shoelaces. I slept with my forearm behind my head on a freezing-cold marble slab shaped like a coffin. A little after sunrise someone passed a pot of extremely hot beef soup through the bars to me; it was in a military-issue canteen cup that I couldn't hold with my bare hands. I let it cool off a little, and I began to feel less chilled as I swallowed the hot liquid. It ran down my throat and slid down my esophagus, the only boiling part of my body— all the rest of me was frozen, chattering bones. Beverly was not there; neither was the old woman with the shawl who used to bring brains and tripe from the slaughter-house in a cart made out of a soda pop box. The old woman helped out in the slaughterhouse every morning, and they gave her livers, kidneys, bits of meat, and pig's feet for free so that she could give them away or sell them on her own from house to house. The black livers, almost dried out, stood out among the other pieces of meat sur-rounded by flies in the cart. Sometimes the livers lay in the backyard for hours at a time while the sweaty, evil-smelling, unwashed old woman, filthy from her daily han-dling of internal organs left sitting in the sun, would sit down with my mother and have a cup of coffee or roast one of those juicy bits. As they gossiped in the kitchen, my father first nailed tin-plate numbers—742—on the house, then nervously smoked a cigarette in the backyard, and then, after a bit, making sure no one saw him leave, took the road downhill past the fallen pirul tree. He took off in the distance toward the dry riverbed with his own peculiar style of pressing his heels down hard against the ground as if he was in a hurry or his gloomy eyebrows were not enough to provide him with a worried and se-rious air, as if all those gestures were not convincing enough to hide the fact that in his heart he felt terrifyingly alone and unprotected. He started walking and then he put on the navy blue jacket he was carrying over his arm, just like the Squadron 201 pilot coming out of the air-plane hangar, and thus, without his typical black suit and his everpresent tie, he scurried away from the house, try-ing to sneak away without being noticed. He was lost from sight and nobody heeded his absence. Sailors in taxis came down through the pass in the hill and got out at the sulfur-water baths on the outskirts of the city, and it was toward the same area that my father fled at sunset.

About the time double-breasted suits began to go out of fashion and the Mexican consul in San Diego gave him a halfdozen or so, he told me as he was shaving in front of the mirror, "I finally have a girlfriend."

He didn't say anything else. He kept looking for a cream or yellow shirt that would go with the brown suit that meant for him, since no one else would guess where they came from, that he was strutting his stuff.

He disappeared again another night, then for whole days at a time; often one or two days would go by without us hearing from him. One afternoon as I was leaving the house on my bicycle in the distance I saw my dad walking toward me. I stopped. He took hold of the handlebars, just looking at me, without speaking. I couldn't say anything. He turned around and left and didn't come home until four in the morning. He knocked on the window. He woke me up with his yelling; his voice was thick, alcoholic, and full of fury and tears.

"Papá . . ."

I opened the door and let him in. I saw him tear off his tie and toss his suit on the sofa—it was his old black suit, well worn, many times ironed, shiny with age—and climb naked into bed. He snored, there in the bed next to mine; his prematurely white beard and his face stuck out of the blanket rolled around his long body like a shroud around a cadaver. I listened to his nicotine-scented snorts. He snored, and from his cheeks, at times, involuntary tics escaped, wiggling his extremely narrow, eaglelike nose, so much like a condor's snot-covered beak. Uneducated, unprepared, not sure of what to do, inventing safety nets, sentimental and submissive, aggressive and discrete, un-

trusting, sad, tender, suspicious, all his love and hate re-
pressed, hungry, jobless, good for nothing. And I think
about him now and again when I saw him leaving a shop
shirtless, with his faded corduroy suit, his baggy pants,
with a net bag of oranges and bananas in one hand. He
was taking big bites out of an apple as if he hadn't eaten
in a week, as if his stomach was aching, with no desire
to greet or speak to anyone.

There was a day, a Sunday morning, when I saw him
lying on the sofa, badly shaven, his legs spread open,
wearing a long, heavy overcoat even though the sun was
shining and it was neither hot nor cold outside. On the
coffee table, on top of the old newspapers and haphaz-
ardly piled magazines, was a glass of grapefruit juice. His
shoes were underneath the table. He crossed one leg over
the other as he sat up, and his pale green velvet hat with
the wide rim framed his face in a grotesque way. A carrot-
colored mustache. He looked like a clown, like an old sad
sack all tired out after the show. He had a cigarette between his lips and was looking in his shirt pocket for a
match. He showed me his varicose veins and told me
about his ulcer. He hunched up suddenly in the chair next
to the bed and put his chin on his knees. He stared at his
toes. He had a red face; his hair was soft and sparse; he
had rounded shoulders and a curved back. He pinched
his cigarette butts between his fingers and dropped them
into a jar of water. Half-eaten sweet rolls littered the table
along with spilt sugar, empty cups, and the dregs of milky
coffee. On one wall hung a trumpet made from an automobile horn with a wooden spool for a mouthpiece.
Standing on the shelf above the bed was a statue of the
Virgin of Carmen with the Christ child in her arms, along
with postcards, newspaper clippings, a picture of the
Agua Caliente tower, and medical prescriptions stuck on

a metal pin. A cardboard box stood half full of pill bottles and used needles. He shut the curtains and didn't go back outside. He began to wear out little by little, disintegrating until his skeleton showed and one could see where his cranial bones joined under his skin. His eyes sunk into his head. As he became thinner, he also became more stretched out and seemed to walk less upright and more slowly. He decided to wait for death, without any hurry, with a certain joy and consoling indifference, without making any effort to speed up the process. He curled up on the bed and, day after day, from one year to the next, drifted into silence.

XVI

Beverly was sleeping on my shoulder when we merged onto the region's main highway. The road entered under the steering wheel, under the two front tires. The sea and the beach fell behind and gradually shrunk backward in the rearview mirror. No one would ever have guessed how cold the Alaskan current really was then.

The afternoons on the coast are chilly; they are as icy as the Pacific, as muted as the Alaskan current that descends along one side of the peninsula until it falls in a curve before Sebastían Vizcaíno Bay. From the tomato fields along the flank of the desert plains one can make out the mountains to one side, the San Pedro Martir chain, and then, far off in the distance, the foamy white, dark blue sea. At some times of the year freighters parade past, sticking close to the shore, but soon they are lost to sight. Only once in a while, every two or three years, the same French ship passes by, leaving the ocean and heading toward the Panama Canal, and it signals the shore with a three-gun salute. A passenger on the deck waves and makes offering signals with his bottle and seems to be saying "Escarpments! The gigantic pinnacles of the Baja California coast, images of aridity and desolation upon which the heart throws itself and is eternally torn apart" (Malcolm Lowry).

A black Piper Comanche circled in the sky. Beverly, weakened, slept on or fell mute. We didn't talk. When the flat part of the beach thinned out into reefs or foam, the earth at the bottom of the precipices turned black. There, between the highway that runs along the coast and the sea, the sand banks are born: small, gentle elevations of sand bathed by the breeze.

We arrived at the beach at dawn, just at the very instant in which the foggy undulations of sand showed the greatest changes in their shifting forms. Up until that time I had been driving the car as if I were part of the machine or its eyes; it was through its eyes, or my bewitched eyes, that the twisted paths detached themselves from the highway. I drove calmly, aware of the proximity of the sea and of Beverly's body at my side. I followed the rest of the cars through the sudden rainstorm that all at once descended like a thick morning fog, and I had to feel my way by looking for the white center line on the asphalt. The heavy fog reduced our visibility to zero. It was impossible to see anything ten meters in front of us. The cars had to take their chances driving blindly over the rain-slickened pavement. Clumsily we followed the sinuous and solitary road as visibility remained practically zero. I opened the window, stuck my head out, grabbed the left side of the steering wheel with my right hand, and drove with my head outside in the wind, my eyes fixed on the white line I could barely make out with one yellow headlight.

"I'm terribly sleepy," said Beverly. "Drive carefully."

I hardly listened to her words. I tried to talk to myself so I wouldn't fall asleep, so that my own eyelids would not blind me.

"Go to sleep," I told her.

Morning began to break.

There was no doubt that we were heading toward the sandbanks, the slightly quicksandlike dunes, isolated white wastelands, piles of exceedingly fine sand awash with water. And to one side of this natural grouping— sky, swamps, clouds, beach—the first triumphant specimen made its appearance before scandalized women and defenseless men. A small plane circled in the sky. Exactly at the curve where the beach disappeared, a tall, strong man emerged from the water—a lifeguard. Now on solid land, taking off his flippers, the tall man made a 4 balancing on one foot. He was wearing orange swimming trunks and he threw down his diving gear. The black specks on the right side of the beach were spectators or seals. The silhouette that began to move forward toward the rocky area was that of the frogman, who was still carrying a pair of flippers in his hand. This arrangement of objects and people was the first thing we saw before us. Beverly and I witnessed the scene from the ledge above, sitting on the fender of the car. The swimmers acclaimed the lifeguard, applauded the hero. They gathered around the spectacle of the seals. More seals came. The audience piled up deeper around the sea species and closed in around them. The oldest seal waved its flipper like a mutilated being, like the body of a man who can barely push himself along on the stumps of his amputated limbs. The upper protuberances—wings, flippers, gelatinous palms—shone when they came in contact with tiny pebbles, bits of mica, foam. Men and women hugged each other, sang, chased each other around, jumped up, threw themselves on the ground. Despite the growing darkness, the lifesaver reappeared and the explosion of applause and cheers very naturally and spontaneously erupted once again. He coldly ignored the ovation; that afternoon he had rescued a woman who now slept wrapped in a blanket in a field tent far from the crowd. Unenthusiastically, the man blended into the crowd of sunbathers and got ready to take part in the nighttime festivities like anyone else.

Joined by the hands like a four-footed monster, we went down the path that led to the beach. We went to see the seals, do you remember, Beverly?

"Yes," she would say, calm, always at my side. "Everything seems less confusing now."

Beverly: her shiny skin toughened now, cheekbones more obviously marked. Go back, look over our footsteps. Clay earth and sand promontories established the border between the beach and our observation point. The dry wind makes us drowsy. We shade our eyes with our hands so we can make out the dispersed features of the distant and evermore diffuse, evermore silent group moving in circles on the beach. In a certain way, the escarpment blends with the piles of rubbish a few meters away from us. The salty weather envelops us in slimy mud, plains, drizzly rain. The sea lions bark playfully, innocently, from the rocky abyss as they float over stagnant water. Little by little their noises establish frequencies, allusions, ancient languages, ciphered messages, words, incomprehensible legends. It's these meows, Beverly, it's these cats that I feel in my gut, this dry sea weather, these fringes delineated by the tidal flux, coves, reefs, harbors, creeks, scarce maritime vegetation, algae, water plants, stubble, collapsed gelatinous spheres of plant life, the coming and going of the waves in the undertow, the underwater life and the estuaries, the smell of shellfish and the deep, heavy dreams in the dunes . . . I only want to preserve the threads of what we provisionally call . . . What do we call it? I'd like to recover interest, to revive a curiosity about the unknown at least.

"I don't want to hurt you. We live in different, divided worlds . . . No, you wouldn't understand . . ."

Endlessly tall Beverly lying on the beach, absently inaccessible, her waist sounding like paint like bitterness, Beverly's damp blonde and chestnut hair falling loose against the path stretching out in the distance, instantaneous movements of her head shaking her hair back.

The road leading down to the sea, the one that leads to the sand piles: sinuous pass after five hours at the wheel; swollen kidneys, one leg asleep. Thickets here and there signal the shortest pass, the straightest cut, and they hide the desert plains that rise up toward the mountains in the center of the peninsula. Hours ago we had driven past a drive-in theater at moderate speed, and we could begin to sense the iodized sea air after passing through the immutably straight line of the Agua Caliente street rising upward toward the hills, which interjected themselves between the most recently developed suburbs of the city and the dikes. Upon returning to one of the roads leading to the old casino, once again, one last time, we refused to recognize the school playgrounds as such, to take cognizance of the crowds of children who, throughout the years, substituted for the elegance and frivolity of previous decades. We made the last inspection in our own way; we would put each thing in its place—the bells in the tower, the cards on the tables, the gambling chips on the roulette boards, the nets on the tennis courts, the lamps in the Salón de Oro, the trays and the wine in the main dining room, the cars aligned perpendicularly with the sidewalk—and we recognized the same trees, the same hotel rooms that, just like before, lined the edges of sunflower carpets and deep hallways, continuing on between one-armed bandits and cashiers' booths right up to the underground gambling rooms. My father scuttled through all these hallways, always trying to escape from the continuous, nerve-racking ticking of the telegraph office, and he wandered from one place to another, from one table to another, from one machine to another, doing whatever he could to lose as soon as possible, just like an obsessive gambler, whatever few coins he jingled in one fist. He dressed very well. No one would have dared to doubt it. He always wore a tie, always wore a vest the same color as his sport jacket—pearl-colored, tobacco-colored, wine-colored—and white Scott Fitzgerald–style shoes. He had a pimple next to his eagle nose and very straight, very black hair. Far away, between demolished walls and a palm tree that barely stood upright, the casino swimming pool made a prominent hole, just like a bomb crater. The mosaics had been torn up, and it was hard to tell the difference between the boiler's rust and the rubble and mud. The diving board made a bridge between one gully and another. We drove around the central ruins of the casino without getting out of the car, and then through the hippodrome ramp and the dried-out golf course of the country club, leaving the casino behind forever. We passed in front of the macabre white public hospital; we got on the highway, avoiding the cemeteries and the automobile junkyards. The old airport for air taxis emerged from the top of the plateau like a postwar military camp but without guards or people anywhere in sight. The remains of the trimotor plane lay crumbling at the hangar entrance, and in the clay courts lined by wire fences, the north end of the tiny closed airport created an ever-stronger contrast with the empty lots in the suburbs. A little later we went up the small slope of Misión del Sol. The cemetery crosses and the knotted highways dissolved at times into a vertiginous Mobius strip that halfway covered the rent-by-the-hour hotels. Men on foot, yellow taxis and other cars left the parking lots in single file. Without any apparent connection, the road next to the beach dipped into the depths of a hollow that abruptly ended at the escarpment. Shells, rocks, coral, chewed watermelon rinds in the sea foam, empty beer cans, old shoes, algae, and stubble marked the intermediate zone between land and sea.

Long before one can glimpse the sea between the mountain peaks, the sand turns into a smooth bit of ground with a few scattered rocks. Rocky caves make the waves echo and a long, rectangular beach enters the scene. We arrive at midnight, when it is barely possible to see the red lights of the high-tension power lines that warn small planes of the danger of flying at low altitudes between the low, spongy clouds. The only traces of life are a few wooden houses and shops: unpainted bungalows corroded by the sun and salty water. We position ourselves at the vantage point of the landscape opened up to us unexpectedly by the end of the pass so as to enjoy this sight for the last time. We stop the car at the escarpment's edge. At that moment, Beverly motions vaguely, without speaking, pointing at an abandoned two-wheeled cart. For a long time we remain silent, seated on the fender of the car watching the sea, the night, the stars, and we only leave when Beverly starts running toward the cart and I follow her. The cart is a goal line, a kind of period, not far, but certain: a tossed stone could hit it. Beverly distances herself from me, with the line of the sea on one side and the surrounding sandbanks on the other. We walk toward the spot that caught our attention over the dunes, heading west, stepping over the bumps in the sand. Once we are lying down under the cart we watch without speaking how the sea swells if we look at it resting a cheek against the ground. At other times of the year these piles are dampened by the breeze and acquire a darker color. The sand darkens and presses in. Anyone could leave footprints by walking along burying their feet.

The seagulls flap their wings, evading the waves' tongues. The sea disappears and returns and backs away. Once again I see from beneath and behind; Beverly is lying down, horizontal; once again I see her on the horseless cart, her head slightly thrown back, a blanket warming her legs. The wind no longer warms, but tears at us coldly and cuttingly. The placidity of the sea becomes uncertain . . . I own the hand that Beverly caresses. I am her only point of support. Release your brakes, come out from your shell, shake yourself, submerge yourself so that you can emerge alive, lift up your protective covering. I sleep on her warm womb, I listen to her stomach gurgle, to her heart beat, and we await the morning freshness, the shock, the gradual descent of sunlight upon our eyes. All at once our faces equalize, we look so much like each other. The breeze blows through, dampening everything, although it more or less seems to float over the passive pleasure of our two sleeping bodies . . . Her first Spanish words: *Susi, ésa es Susi, Susi se asea* . . . In another mood we might have been compelled to throw ourselves over the cliff; a less tense tranquillity, another time might have suggested the idea of rolling down the undulating waves of sand. The sandbanks would hide us, would prepare our bed in the crater's depths, and we would continue sleepily dozing there below.

I get up. I stop to look at the shadows my eyes detect on the horizon. Beverly rests in the horseless cart, a lock of hair covering her forehead. She touches her face with her hand and the hair enveloping her forces her to bat her eyelashes too frequently.

"Put a finger under your eye and press inward," I tell her, "and you'll see me divided into twin faces."

I zigzag along the edge of the foam left behind by the waves. But before that I climb down the escarpment, jumping from rock to rock, and I reach the soft part of the beach.

Tall and mute, Beverly. Mute from the moment in which she undertakes the trip to the coast with me. We cross a mountain; the pass has vestiges of a cemetery at its peak. The highway stretches all along its length, down below. Up above, the moldy tombs in no way dissimulate the few bony remains still there. It is on this particular bit of road that Beverly goes mute.

Dawn finds us asleep. I wake up and go down toward the sea. Beverly sleeps profoundly on the cart which, ex-posed to sun and salt, looks even drier and more fragile than before. I take off my shoes. I shuffle in the sand. I run around without taking account of the chilly sea foam at my feet. I don't back up. I hear smothered screams at my back, from the direction of the escarpment. After two or three steps I turn around and run back anxiously, and when I begin to get closer I discover that the part of the beach where the cart was has been swallowed up between the rocks and the water. Beverly is nowhere in sight. I look, I search, I trace my footsteps backward, enormously upset. I run across the flat surface and scream for help. Far away, on a stone pathway, the lifeguard returns after having ostentatiously accomplished another rescue. I yell at him, but he can't hear me. Behind a campfire lit inside

a rubber tire, a group of people admire the seals' show. I walk into the water up to my knees and grab the woman farthest from the group by the shoulder.

"If I die, what will you think of me?"

The woman cannot restrain her laughter. She immediately turns her head and makes a face at me, inviting me. I smile and I explain with my hands, gesturing toward the enthusiastic excitement that animates the show, that it is impossible for me to participate now.

"I need a crane," I beg her.

The other members of the audience pay no attention to my interjections. In the center of the circle made by linked arms and hands there stands the figure of an iron seal with damp skin. It suddenly takes on the shape of a huge, recently emptied statue; later it dresses in a Polichinella's multicolored costume and still later it rolls itself up in a heavy black cape. The seal rises upward, tossing the cape back over its chest proudly, a black mass, sweet burned iron. On my knees, I feel my bittersweet tongue against the sand and water that cover its metallic surface. I lick the seal's arms. Sweetly, sweetly, I let my tongue play in the folds of the cape. The giant remains upright, fixed to its pedestal, impermeable to the shower of the waves. The seal is twice the size of an average man, and a child has climbed up on its back. The child is holding an orange in one hand and he offers it, extending his arm forward. The child and the seal are parts of the same sculpture. The child is a prolongation of the seal's shoulder, its webbed fingers, its fish-shaped body, its doglike head and neck, covered with grey hair, sparse and soaked; the child also forms part of its right breast, and both are surrounded by a fine, shiny, hairy skin. They're wet. Thus the child contorts himself inside the oldest seal, or the seal moves its right shoulder. Men and women take each

other's hands. They dance and sing around the statue: *Naranja dulce limón partido dame un abrazo que yo te pido*—sweet orange sliced lemon give me a hug I beg of you . . .

One of the women threatens to invite me. I bring my hands to my mouth. I rub them over my sweaty forehead. I look behind me; a crane is pulling the cart out of the water, the light and Pegasus-free cart, its moldy wheels damp. Beverly: dark chestnut hair dripping over her face that emerges covered with algae and pieces of bandage. The crane places her body on a gauze sheet and all at once she is again lying in the cart. I dry her face with a towel and geraniums fall from the crane's great chain. Beverly opens her eyes without seeing me. I hold out my hand, separating my fingers, I fan them in front of her eyes. I move my body; I move my face from one side to another. Beverly does not follow me with her gaze. Her eyes remain focused on a midway point in some imprecise location of sky or night.

By the time the sun has finally made an appearance, I have Beverly's belongings stored in the car.

"I'll drive," I tell her. "You sleep."

She is no less mute than before when I take her with me, at my side, always next to me, like a part of my own body that refuses to detach itself. She seems to doze as she slips down against my right shoulder when we leave the pass and take the region's main highway. We go up the coastline on the new freeway. Without going into the city we take the road that runs parallel to the fence at the international border. There are very few cars in line at this time of day. The border guard asks to see our documents, and I show him my multiple-entry visa. He asks for hers. I tell him that she's sleeping right now. In a fraction of a second, or perhaps less, I see her at my side again, and I recall the previous few minutes when I had been driving on the coastal road watching the sea and the beach fall behind us in my rearview mirror. The officer doesn't wait for me to articulate my sudden misgivings and insistently demands to see her passport one more time. He yells at me to wake her up. I tell him she is sick. He insists on speaking to her. I touch her arm, but Beverly doesn't react. Then I feel something cold soaking my pants. I squeeze my eyes shut in an effort to erase the image of a bullfighter with wounded thigh that suddenly appears in the momentary darkness of my closed eyes. In that way, with my eyelids shut, I feel my two legs and Beverly's thigh resting next to mine. The officer's awkward shove on Beverly's shoulder shakes me out of my lack of awareness. Beverly's body suddenly tips to the right and the blood is there, fresh and spreading wider underneath her thighs. On my hands. I don't touch anything else. I don't touch the steering wheel. I remain with my hands out, paralyzed. Pallid, stiff, Beverly rests at my side, without breathing.

XVII

And now, and now here I am sitting in my room. I've cleaned off all the walls; I no longer have any paintings up, I haven't stuck up a single photograph. I remember I used to like to stick posters up on walls, but lately I have been wanting to live in a clean room, I want to know what it feels like to live within white walls. I didn't choose the color of the walls; that's the way they were. It's a clean room, a clean bed, a closet made of rough wood, it's unpainted and beautiful. A plain lamp, a desk, a window; the window looks out on a leafy spot, has a view of a cliff and rustic countryside through which a river once flowed.

During the night I can hear the cars driving down the highway off in the distance, on the other side of the pirul trees that lead down to the beach. And sometimes I can also hear the footsteps of someone walking through the leaves, and from this part of the city, the city itself seems to be filled with luminous points, with lights, because this part of town is dark and has no electricity. And the airplane engines buzz as the planes fall softly over the airport when a certain shift in the wind forces them to land from this direction. And some lost airplane makes me leap out of bed at midnight and stick my head out the window and stare up at the sky . . . And at the bottom of the hill the chain fence between the two countries comes to an end and it forms a corner through which the northern part of the valley cuts. And seagulls stop their squawking as night falls and then the sea blackens against the also black sky . . . But it is impossible for you to contemplate these places again. The sea has swept away the traces of the Piper Comanche that left you on the tiny landing strip that first time. And we were frightened, we were very frightened, and the black clouds were no more than the continuation of the mountains seen against the backdrop of the dying sun, the absolute night that surrounded everything hid our actions from the world and evaded foreign presences in this precise spot on the beach at the outermost limits of the land belonging to the Agua Caliente casino. We were frightened, we were sitting at the top of the slope contemplating the sea, in that very site and, I don't know how to tell you this, Beverly, I know that I act clumsily in trying to bring you back to me, even in a veiled manner. And I disperse myself and I wallow in my own incongruencies as if you had never left me with a perfectly delineated impression of your face, of your way of being and moving that allowed me to feel alive once again, Go to the corner and buy an ice cream, you told me, and I ran out in a rush to get that cone, squeezing the coin that you had taken out of your purse, and I ran back with the almost-melted scoop of ice cream so that I could share it with you, and now, now it doesn't matter what part of the world I find myself in, I have turned up in places I know nothing about and I drive around as if I had lived there my whole life, and I live alone, it's all the same to me, I live halfway, I speak in a minor key, I don't think *I am* anywhere; when it gets right down to it, all I care about is eating and sleeping, in halftones, that's the way I hear noises, that's the way I speak, that's the way I listen to music. And I'm not even moved by symphonies, and I could talk for hours on end about anything, with anybody, and I'm not bored in the slightest by the most habitual behavior. And at times I am very afraid of dying, but with ten hours of sleep my nerves relax and my glands relax. And I get up to eat, I shower because it doesn't take any extra effort—there's hot water in my room at all hours—and I gaze at myself in the mirror because I don't recognize myself and because the mirror is there and because I can't avoid it. And ever since I was born I have been chewing on my fingernails, I never let them grow, I must have digested tons of nail clippings since I was born and I began to chew bits of my body; maybe they've settled in my stomach by now and covered it with a whitish layer or maybe with another crust on the cerebral cortex where, they say, the seat of language resides. I believed that you didn't want to eat, that you didn't need to eat, that you had no desires and so, in that way, covertly, cautiously, on guard, I've allowed the years to slip by. My words are not my words; I use terminology that means nothing to me, or that changes meaning as the years pass, or that dilutes itself in a diction that no longer serves even me; words lose themselves gutturally and I have no option left but to fall silent as you fell silent, although your muteness always belonged to another, and equally insubstantial, order (or disorder) of ideas, they're words that I've heard frequently and suddenly I surprise myself, I catch myself in flagrant and stupid lies, saying something in a certain way, and then the realization that it is not me who is speaking immediately shuts me up. Maybe I am not even the person who opens his mouth and moves his lips and swallows saliva and tightens his stomach and feels the inclement stretching of all the digestive pathways. But the truth is that I do it all without raising my voice, I'm very careful in that respect, I speak in a very low whisper and I write longhand so as not to disturb anyone's hearing; I'm very embarrassed to be here talking, forgive me for making noise. I confess; I confess to being here, before the whole world, the world ceases its spinning and its displacement through the universe, and I hope that in some way, that is, someday, really, I'm not bothering anyone, yes, I beg your pardon for being here, I don't know, maybe you have something else more important to do, as soon as possible I will disappear, whatever you say, whenever is convenient for you, I'm here to serve you, it's just that I thought, it's just that

Anticipating Incorporation

My mother and I never got along well. An only son with two sisters, I soon came to realize that I was trapped in enemy territory. The battle was lost in advance; I escaped as often as I could from that house soaked from its very foundations in the tastes, the style, and the gazes of all the women who surrounded my mother.

In those days she tried not to talk much about her husband. He was practically invisible in any case, with his presence concentrated in the noisy evenings and early mornings of coffee and alcohol. The streets, meanwhile, had become impassable. Muggings and gang violence, my inability to incorporate myself into extramural basketball clubs, the threat of the Free Frays, the Pegasuses, the Dragons—they all contributed to my ever-stricter isolation and daily sense of enclosure. A little later on, at the end of the summer, I found myself inside the Tres Estrellas de Oro, where, after crossing the bridge over the Rodríguez Dam, I was torn—for the first and possibly last

time—out of the adolescent Tijuana that I did not know
how to make my own.

The high white curtain of the dam, so like an impen-
etrable castle wall, marked a point of departure, a definitive and perhaps premature separation. In the Tecate
striations, off to one side of Matanuco's vineyards and
interminable olive groves, terrain was becoming green in
some sections barely brushed by a miserly rain. The majestic white rocks looked as if they were newly sprinkled
over the landscape, separated from each other by the pre-
historic volcanic vomit of the mountains that faded away
in the dark and purple distance of the horizon. I probably
fell asleep as we wound through the Rumorosa ascents
and descents. Hours later the night in all its splendor and
silence, the open and starry sky—these things lulled me
into a soft meditative state, like a daydream, that on the
one hand set before me the enigma of a city like Hermosillo, and on the other hand left behind me the sudden
certain appearance of my father at the bus station: he
would give me a pack of gum just after my mother put
the bus ticket into my hand. I remembered him, nevertheless, in his moments of exaltation and talkativeness:
his unexpected intrusion into the house as we all slept,
the violent brightness of all the lights coming on, his ramblings, his unstoppable monologues imposed upon us in
shouts and tense pauses, his compulsive need to have a
cup of coffee.

The orange desert sunrise made all these impressions
·very tenuous. The half-sleep sweetly interrupted by the
straight road and infrequent curves, the pleasant passivity of feeling myself transported and the sensation of insufficient sleep: these things added up to the passage between night and day, to the 'recuperation' of my home, to
warm milk and games with my sisters, and to the fallen

pirul tree in the crevice where we used to hide, but at the same time they foretold of an inevitable, although potentially momentary, hell that I was unable to explain. I felt that I was lying down in the world.

Sedated by the effects of light on the window, by the quiet of the cacti and of nodding heads, I shook myself awake and focused on contemplating the immediate future, guessing if I could, whether or not that distant Hermosillo, rooted in the desert plain, would fulfill my fears or my preconceptions.

It was as if the city had been evacuated. Around four o'clock in the afternoon people locked the doors of their houses. Nobody was in the streets. The sunflowers bent their heads, beaten, burned. Hot air, successive waves of wind, an unlocatable fire weighed down the atmosphere, but before nightfall the unpaved roads were inundated by water from the pipes that emerged unpredictably from the dust far away and extended toward us—slow, heavy, and generous. It smelled of damp earth, and the ground was yellowish as I walked down Garmendia Street. I was going to the movies. I was sweating. The midnight show revived an intimate capacity for illusion in me. Soon September would come, the enrollment period would end, and high school classes would start.

And then I started my military service.

We presented ourselves in the barracks on the first Sunday in January. We began drills even before the sun came up. We were more than a thousand chilly and overtired men, and we were the only living beings in that peaceful city. We marched in rows of four, without weapons or uniforms, recent recruits called up for an improbable general mobilization. We marched in front of the stairs of the museum and the public library, looking for an exit into the open air. The museum's enormous stairway and stone columns made it look like something from imperial Rome. Then the order came down. We had to run at top speed. Before we realized it, the houses on the outskirts of the city began to fall behind us at the same time as the dawn began to break in the sky.

The dry, flat valley extended forever. We were divided into groups, each group under the charge of a sergeant. The morning was spent doing calisthenics and marching, and around noon we received the order to concentrate along a boundary that represented the borderline between the cotton fields and the irrigation channel. Major Dorantes climbed on top of a promontory. An olive green canvas bag hung from one shoulder, like that of a clumsy mail carrier who waited soberly before our expectant eyes on the battlefield. With one eye on us and one on the list that a sergeant was unfolding in front of him, Major Dorrantes shouted out our military designations. One by one, alternately, we took a step forward, and first coming to attention and then saluting, we picked up our military cards as the major pulled them out of the canvas bag. Those of us who were under eighteen got ours last: Soldier's name. Registration number 421363-2. Anticipating incorporation according to regulation number 54069, file D/143/184453, June 30, 1960 (application attached). Department of Military Identification and Recruitment. Ministry of National Defense. National Military Service. Class 1943.

"Who knows how to play the drums or the trumpet?"

"I do," I lied, without intending to. In those days I thought that I could do anything, that I could do everything I never dared to or wasn't ready to try before. And so it was that every Sunday we left the regiment to give shape to a strident and cacophonous military band. We took turns in the honor guard: some of us played while others slept or took naps in the cotton fields until one of the sergeants came and told us to go back to the barracks.

It was still dark outside when we rushed from our various locations across the city to get to our first early-morning high school class. Silent and recently awakened, we all converged on the lawn from which the building's first nave detached itself. Above our early-morning indifference a sign in copper-colored mosaic spelled out the indecipherable maxim: Maximum liberty within maximum order.

Around noon, as school emptied out, the customary dispersion of the group took on another quality. We walked in herds. We stopped for sodas.

"I've always grown up around women," I told Graciela and Laura.

"We'll take care of you," said Graciela.

We caught a glimpse of Jacinto Astiazarán, with his crew cut on top and the rest of his hair shaved around the ears, as he revved up his Islo motorbike as if it were a Harley-Davidson. He was wearing a black leather jacket with a sheepskin collar. His dark glasses made him look more serious, introspective, and interesting as he pulled on his suede gloves. Alone, always alone, always the lone ranger who shot off noisily across the plain on his motorbike.

After saying good-bye to Laura and Graciela, I looked at the imposing hump of the museum and public library that was the highest point in the city outside Campana Peak. I felt ever smaller and more insignificant as I came closer to the stairway, as if I ought to take a deep breath before taking on one step at a time, before facing the challenge of those columns that inevitably evoked Rome. The two enormous side wings converged in straight vertical lines, falling at a guardrail that protected the statue of General Abelardo Rodríguez. Several students who were still trying to concentrate on their reading sought out the freshness of the shadows in the hallways. I went into the periodicals room. I put my books on a table and began to look through the newspapers from Baja California that arrived two or three days late. I picked up a Thursday paper. It was Saturday. A small article buried in the back of the paper froze my blood. I rushed to pick up my books and took off running down the museum stairs with no goal in mind. Down below I saw Jacinto Astiazarán organizing military drills with the Pentatlón commandos. They were howling and smacking the ground with their goose-step march. They jogged around and followed Jacinto Astiazarán, who stood straight and tall in his leather jacket, dark glasses, blue jeans, and tall black riding boots, down there below me in that field, in that movieesque Zeppelinfeld from Nuremberg.

I got out of school at 12:30. At 12:45 I was in the periodicals room.

I flipped through the newspapers from Tijuana. I read the front pages. I glanced through the middle sections. There, below, in a corner: FORMER TELEGRAPHER KNIFED.

At 1:10 I ran down the museum steps. At 1:15 I wandered the streets, without any precise goal in mind. At 3:00 someone on the bus station sidewalk stuck a ticket in my hand. And I went. At 6:00 I was crossing the desert in a very cold red bus. At midnight the bus climbed the peaks of Rumorosa.

At 5:00 the next morning I entered the Tijuana public hospital.

His prematurely grey beard stuck out over the sheets; his forehead and eyes were exactly like mine. Excitement and cigarettes were strictly forbidden. He had never seen me smoke before. I approached his bed with a cigarette in my hand. He asked me for a drag. He smoked for a little while, and he smiled. I kissed him on the forehead.

I went out in the hallway to continue smoking. The Agua Caliente casino's silhouette began to take on a sharper contrast against the sunset. From time to time I stuck my head in his room. He was sleeping peacefully, as calm and restful as a child.

My mother and one of my sisters showed up in the hallway many hours later.

"We didn't know you were here."

"Why didn't you let me know?"

I went back to Hermosillo.

"Shit," said the major. "We've got to try to help each other out. I'll give you two Sundays for every goat skin you bring me. Look at them—out of fifteen drums, twelve are broken. Do what you can to fix the drum skins; put the bottom skin on top and leave the top skin, attach it however you can, run the cords over the ripped part."

I missed a lot of soldiering sessions. Some absences added up because of summer Sundays, vacations, and mornings I just couldn't seem to wake up on time, others because of my unexpected trip to Tijuana. In similar circumstances other guys had to come back and drill the next year.

"Two Sundays for each goat skin," the major had told me.

So one morning I went to the outskirts of Hermosillo, in the direction of Villa Seris, with the drum hoops in my hands.

"We don't have any here," they told me at one ranch.

"What did you say you were looking for?" asked an old man.

"Goat skins."

"No, not here."

Toward the south there was an adobe house with a brick tower next to it. A woman was washing clothes and hanging them on a barbed wire fence. As I came up to her I saw a cracked landing strip in the distance and I noticed a small rusted searchlight on top of the tower.

"I don't know if they ought to be tanned or not," I told her.

"I have these," answered the woman, pointing to some hard, greasy things hanging over the fence and baking in the sun. "But they have hair on them."

"Fifty pesos?"

"It's a deal."

They were covered in a layer of fat. I began sticking them into a concrete sink full of hot water. I stuck the hoops on a long, wooden, fly-speckled bench. The woman was barefoot and her dress was damp in parts. She had a huge copper pot boiling away and she threw powdered soap into the pot and stirred the pants with a long pole.

"A scraper. Ma'am, do you happen to have a scraper?"

The woman went into the house and came back out. Her hands were wet and she held out a moldy old scraper and a red shaving blade in two pinched fingers.

"Great. Listen, thanks," I told her. Then there was a long pause, a silence. "You don't have any children?"

"They're around. They like to take off into the hills."

I went closer to her and without saying a word dumped a pail of hides into her pot of soapy water. One by one the multicolored, shapeless rawhides softened in the hot water. The woman helped by rescuing the steamy hides from the hot water with her pole. She stretched them out on the bench next to the hoops, and the scraper stickily fought its way through the soapy skins. Bits of grease kept slipping away between the hairs and the flies when I felt something burning between two of my fingers.

"Laura . . ."

"Why are you calling me Laura?"

"No, it's just that . . . it looks like I cut myself."

Blood ran down my forearm in streams. The woman rinsed her hands, shook them out, and finished drying them off on her skirt.

"Come here," she told me.

Inside the house a hammock hung across the room from one wall to the opposite one, held up by two buried tree trunks.

"It's my sister's name," I told her hesitantly.

"Sit down here."

I waited, sitting in the hammock. She disappeared through the only door that led out back. All alone, I looked around and was able to make out a sawed-off shotgun under a cot and, above the headboard, a Moctezuma Brewery calendar. On the shelf above, a candle tenuously illuminated a small picture of the Virgin of Carmen and a man's photograph.

She came back carrying a bronze wash jug on top of a big bowl, and I felt compelled to tell her something . . . but I kept quiet. I remained with my arm stiff, held straight up, and my hand loose, the elbow cupped in my other palm. The blood between my fingers had coagulated. The woman then pushed a little stool in front of me with her foot, right about knee height, and she sat down with the bowl in her lap. She took my wrist and held my hand gently over the white pewter of the bowl while she poured warm water over it from the jug. With the pads of her fingers she softened the bloody crust on mine. She brought a recently ironed towel that smelled like sunshine to dry it; after that she opened a bottle of Mercurochrome.

"No, it's OK as it is," I told her.

She watched me go out into the yard and let me pick up the goat skins as best I could with one hand. I began lining them up on the drum frames. They were still dripping and they were smeared with grease, but they took the shape of the circumference required of them. I heard a stream of running water at my back; the woman washed off the scraper, and then she picked up the razor blade and came toward me.

"Watch out," she said. She jabbed the knife into one of the skins and cut across it from right to left and around the circumference of the drum head, leaving a piece to overlap the edge of the hoop. She repeated her perfect cuts on the goat skins that were beginning to dry out and change from brown to a shade of white. The hoops tightened and resisted the stretching and shrinking of the skins under the sun. We went to rest in the shade. On the long bench the five circular skins lined up in strict military order.

The military band headed the column of the National Military Service's First Infantry Battalion at around eleven o'clock on the morning of September 16. We marched double-time to take up our positions along Serdán Avenue. For the first and last time we felt on our shoulders the weight of a Mauser with a bayonet fixed to it. During the slack time, while the school contingents and other groups took their turns heading down the parade route, we remained at ease, smoking and eating jicamas and cucumbers with lemon. We drummers and trumpeters had red braid and tassels to make us stand out from the rest of the company. We were straightening out our equipment and putting the last touches on our regulation tricolor cockades when, all at once, all by himself, Jacinto Astiazarán came around the corner swallowed up in a cadet's blue violet uniform that had faded almost to grey, almost white, almost steel-colored. Several seconds went by before the Pentatlón honor guard spun into sight with a ninety-degree turn and marched along parallel to our company and followed by five platoons of Pentatlonians. Distanced from his troups by a space of at least ten meters, Jacinto Astiazarán marched stiffly erect, carrying a silver saber lined up with his nose, equidistant between his two eyebrows and held at the level of his cap. The Pentatlón members all wore black shirts and tight white pants. They had precisely matched white helmets as well, and parachute netting, and each proudly controlled a machine gun held at waist level.

Following the first trumpet call we took our places behind the Pentatlón group and thundered down the avenue. The beating of the drums filled the street and made the crowd rush back onto the sidewalk. With every step forward, the drum slapped against my left leg; I pushed it back at an angle where I could reach and balance it with my drumsticks. I watched my companions out of the corner of my eye so as to keep the line straight. A few meters away, in the middle of the crowd on my right, I could see out of the corner of my eyes my mother waving a pink handkerchief at me, smiling, her mouth lipsticked bright red. I greeted her with my eyes while trying to keep my head facing front. I got out of step for a moment. I lowered my gaze and saw, to one side of the drum, my wool uniform pants, just like John Wayne's on the beach at Iwo Jima. I would have liked to have been a U.S. Marine, I had bought myself some identical uniform pants in the secondhand shop in San Isidro, and I also bought a helmet on which I later painted the lieutenant's white bars . . . I slung my rifle across my chest as I crouched down and my sister took my picture, and a white hole underneath the zipper showed clearly under the olive green canteen strap . . . My mother started to follow us along the parade route, but I lost sight of her in the crowds. Once we had marched in front of the city hall, our column veered down Centenario Avenue and we headed back toward the barracks. We returned the Mausers, left the drums in the storeroom, and dispersed. Few draftees remained on the streets. I walked down the sidewalk with my equipment in my arms, and there on the boulevard she was waiting on an empty iron bench.

"What a shock! I never imagined that you might show up around here. I felt as if my pants were falling down."

"You looked very handsome. And then with the rifles. I never imagined that you would show up right there in the band. Who would believe it?"

"So you've come to rescue me from a life of crime."

"I didn't say that."

We went to eat in a Chinese restaurant.

"Too bad there's no duck."

"Back home there is," she said.

The waitress brought us several dishes: fried rice, tofu, sweet-and-sour spareribs.

"Look, do it this way. First the bottom one, like holding a pencil; then the top one, as if you were writing. Like a pigeon's beak."

"I've been thinking that you might come home with me. I don't know what you're doing here. Back home you could continue your studies, in San Diego. Now that your sisters have gone. And your dad . . . I don't know what to do alone in the house. It's not like I didn't want to write to you. Do you remember?"

"I remember perfectly."

"You look furious for some reason. And then they say to me, 'Listen Marianita, what's your kid doing there leaning against the door of the shop at all hours of the night, until closing time, and he never goes to bed until really late.' It's not that I forgot about you. It's just that it wasn't easy. Your father . . . poor man. You didn't catch on to things. And that day when the school bus dropped us off at the corner, and we got out. Why? What had you done? That girl—what was her name?—she was a student of mine and, no, I did not like one bit what you used to say from one window to another, and you so young. But it was all foolishness, I know that now. I shouldn't have said anything to you until we got home. I shouldn't have hit you in front of her, in front of everyone on the bus. I felt really bad about it later. You don't know how bad, I could never tell you about it . . ."

"No, it was nothing . . ."

"You can keep going there. Everything is there. You'll fit right back in. Vacation will be over in a flash and you will go back to school. The girls rarely come to see me."

"In a while I want to go to Mexico City."

"Sure, later, whenever you want. It's only for a couple of years; there's lots of time for all that. Until I get used to it. But it's got to be now. I can't go on like this . . . We'll go to the beach to eat lobster."

"But why does it have to be this very instant? Just now when I'm starting out?"

"Gordo, I don't have anyone left," she said, and there was a long silence.

"Do you want some more tea?"

"That's enough, no sugar."

We sat without talking. I rubbed my barracks identification with my fingertips, without saying a word. I refilled my cup with tea. Flavorless. Cold. With one of the chopsticks she moved a few leftover grains of rice around on the plate. We refused to look each other in the eye.

"Where's your luggage?"

"At the station." A pause. "Do you like it here?"

"Yes."

"Will you come to see me whenever you can?"

"Always." Silence.

"Eat well. Don't stay up late. Write me, for whatever you need."

"Sure."

"We ought to ask for the bill."

We walked along underneath the Indian laurel trees following the shadows on the street. We went into the bus terminal. She gave me her locker key. I took out her suitcase.

"Here," she told me.

"What is it? Oh. Hey, what made you think of this?"

It was a pair of new shoes in a box.

I walked her to the Tres Estrellas de Oro platform.

"And don't be so lazy," she told me. "Get up early."

She seemed to just naturally move her head from one side to another and to blink her eyes every now and again.

Not another word. She climbed on the bus and went to sit in the back without looking out at me. I raised my hand, but I couldn't see her behind the tinted windows.

I left the terminal with my hands in my pockets and the shoebox under my arm. The bus headed over the damp yellow earth toward the outskirts of town in a cloud of dust that rose up and then dissipated. It disappeared in the distance, roaring down the highway. I walked on alone down Garmendia Street.

Tijuana Times

remember them all very well: Oki, Tavo, Pilucho, Chavo, Oscar, Yuca, Kiki, Juan, Kiko, Pelón. Or maybe not; I must be forgetting a few names. How could anyone forget Mickey Banuet? They were really good at basketball, at fistfights, at kicking people around. If it weren't for the Free Frays, the Romandía, the Matus, the Cachuchas Insunza, the Pegasuses would have been the best basketball players of their time. They were the terror of the Cacho neighborhood, the Sombrero, the Country Club. They'd show up at parties all at once in their custom Fords with chrome pipes—like James Dean's black Mercury—in their pickups with the front ends jacked up, with their red jackets with the white leather sleeves and the name "Pegasus" embroidered on the backs and a winged horse like Mobil Oil's below the lettering.

They came from some of the best Tijuana families, but not the really strict ones. They hung out at night. They toured the poor parts of town, but never strayed into the outskirts of the city or into enemy territory. Sometimes

they would condescend to allow members of other gangs
to join them and link up with the group—the guys that
were fun, or good at basketball, or not afraid of a fight,
like Mickey Banuet. And they'd tend to gang up on a single adversary and beat him up all together once they got
him down on the ground. Up on one of the hills, on the
other side of the television peak or in the Chapultepec
neighborhood, they would organize ritual Bacchic cele-
brations. They would bring an enormous tub full of beer
and ice up the hill in the trunk and sing Fats Domino's
"On Blueberry Hill." The Pegasus Club. That's what they
called themselves. A Jesuit priest had organized it as part
of his project involving working with young people, especially those from rich families.

Tijuana was a livable city in those days. Its inhabitants
still fit very well between the mountains that surrounded
it. During one of those years James Dean smashed himself up on the highway and Marlon Brando raced motor-
cycles or treated his swollen eyebrows on the New York
docks. Those were the days of phosphorescent socks and
tight, greasy Levis, of boots and shoes with taps. Bill Ha-
ley reached us through the Hit Parade of a San Diego
radio station. And Perry Como: "Hot Diggity." And Tab
Hunter: "Young Love, First Love," etcetera . . . And Elvis
Presley, of course: "You Ain't Nothing But a Hound Dog"
. . . And Little Richard: "Tutti Frutti," "Good Golly, Miss
Molly" . . .

And on the other side, the Escuderos, the Free Frays,
and the Seventeen hung out. You had to choose colors,
to belong to a gang in order to be somebody. An orange
or black jacket with sleeves of white or sky blue or purple
with yellow polka dots was all it took. You couldn't walk
around alone. The streets were dangerous, the parties a

place for prickly emotions and offense-taking—a kind of hidden class war.

It wasn't easy to get into any of the clubs and it was hard to figure out which was the right one to join, maybe because all the members were three or four years older, or maybe because you didn't try hard enough. The fact is that solitary barrio nights were filled with dreams of belonging to the Pegasuses. And why not? They had everything: cars, jackets, girlfriends, power, class, prestige in sports. They were the city's bosses and you'd watch them go by with mixed feelings of admiration and rancor.

Those were the days when people got beat up in the middle of the street, the days of getting weighed (a friendly, ironic, humiliating mugging), and you would die of fear whenever you had to go downtown alone and you ran into Memín, Jorgillo, or the *chucos* from other neighborhoods who piled up around the area of the Roble Theater or in the lower part of Bujazán on Sundays.

The Korean War had just ended. Once in a while you'd hear that some mother from the Coahuila or Libertad neighborhood received the useless homage of a posthumous purple heart for a son killed in battle. It was not uncommon to see a dull-colored olive green Chevy, like MacArthur's, heading up into the hills in a cloud of dust carrying the official notification of that absurd medal.

It wasn't true that you could sweep up the dollars with a broom, but Tijuana was a party town. Sometimes the natives dared to sneak into the Waikiki, the Blue Fox, the Aloha, or the Ballena, more out of curiosity than any real desire to mingle with the dancers and the Yankee sailors.

I was born and grew up on Río Bravo Street, right in front of the Pensador Mexicano School. In our neighborhood we played baseball with the guys on Top against the guys on the Bottom, but the designations were pragmatic ones having more to do with geography than with any other kind of rivalry. Along Río Navas, the street descended sharply and the dry riverbed began. Our differences weren't like those between black and white. They lived in the most extreme poverty, and we barely made it into a kind of lower-middle class, and certainly never into the upper class, where the Pegasuses flew in their happy world. Nevertheless, you could still ask yourself if everybody, that is, if the Tops and the Bottoms all had the same opportunities, the same advantages. A lot of them emigrated to Los Angeles. Some stayed. One died in Vietnam. The luckiest ones were those who got a chance to go to one of the universities.

The Rodríguez Reservoir began to dry up around that time, perhaps as the involuntary signal that the epoch of prosperity was coming to an end. The fifties slipped by, and with the passage of time, old friends gradually dispersed, the clubs wore down and fell apart. The colors on the jackets faded and the leather sleeves lost their pristine white color. Pilucho, Kiko and Yuca went on to study law in Mexico City. Oscar got into hunting and pigeon shooting. Mickey Banuet showed up less and less often in the northern zone cantinas. I never heard what happened to the rest. Once I ran into Chavo Villanueva, who was with Rogelio Gastelúm in the Benjamin Hill train station or some other place in the Sonora Desert, but I never saw or heard anything else about him. And who could ever forget Mickey Banuet? Where are you, Mickey Banuet? What have you done with your life?

Many years earlier, between World War II and the Korean War, my mother taught at Pensador School, my father was still in the telegraph office, and my sisters were already working. We used to hang out in the barrio: the

Valenzuela brothers (Ernesto, Oscar, and Armando), their cousin Federico Sáinz, and me. We clearly belonged to a Tijuana of no more than a hundred thousand inhabitants. Sometimes we went to Puerta Blanca Stadium to see the Potros and Bacatete Fernández. Later on, as we got older, we went to hunt birds with 22-caliber rifles in the dry riverbed, next to the fallen pirul tree. Federico Sáinz always bought us Pepsis, ice cream, and apples; he was generosity, kindness, and enthusiasm personified. Sometimes the *chucos* came down from other neighborhoods. Once they came from Libertad, crashed a wedding, and kicked Zambo to death. We well-off kids from the rising middle class intuited that there were two different ways of life represented in the difference between the hills and the valley plain, that there were innumerable Tijuanas superimposed upon each other, that fate often found victims. It was an adolescent Tijuana. The gregarious wish to identify oneself with a club was a survival strategy, the need to be part of something at any cost, the desire to belong.

Then came junior high school at the Tech, the mysterious fire in the Agua Caliente tower, and Santiago Ortega, Ricardo Gilbert, and Memo Díaz, and then there were Marta Franco, Elsa Apango, Alma Marín, and, oh, ah, Celia Santamaría and the dances in the Salón de Oro. And time marched on. Like imperfect and human parallel lines, our biographies briefly touched during a very short period of time, and afterward they separated into infinity. Not even memories and affection from long ago are enough to recuperate the lived life. You are your past and your present at the same time, but the future had already passed us by and we didn't even realize it.

Now Tijuana has a million inhabitants. There are only a few people left from the old days: some, a very few, of those who were born and grew up here. Alongside the inexplicable opulence, there are people who survive in the hills and canyons in huts dangerously built upon foundations of old tires. Conditions haven't changed; the outlines have, though. On one hand, in the city full of masters of ceremonies, clubs proliferate. Parties and weddings take place among clouds of dry ice and real trees, just like in the best days of the Agua Caliente casino. On the other hand, like the *chucos* excluded from the banquet, the *cholos* multiply, their long plaid shirts buttoned at the neck and hanging loose over khaki pants.

Pilucho, Tavo, Kiko, and Yuca are now distant presences, but in their radiant and youthful times, they seemed like the life that was slipping through our fingers.

"Where have you been, in Los Angeles?"

The question presupposes a myth. Every absence is related to an adult destiny on Los Angeles's East Side. When you come back from whatever part of the world, more than thirty years later, and especially in May, you'll see that the Rodríguez Dam is about to overflow and that the hills on the outskirts are covered in green. Some names extinguish themselves in your memory, and others reappear among the police or government officials. But where is Mickey Banuet? Who could ever forget Mickey Banuet?

Los Brothers

Laura and I had already decided to break off our relationship though we didn't talk about it during those last few weeks. One Saturday afternoon I entered the apartment and discovered that all her things were gone. She didn't leave a note; that wasn't her style, and besides, we hadn't been talking to each other at that stage.

The next morning, after having slept far more than necessary, I went to the pizzeria next door, longing for some black coffee to wake me up, just like that, definitively. It was a very foggy Sunday. Almost the whole northern part of the city was dark. You couldn't figure out whether it was raining or not. You never know. I was sitting in one of the metal chairs that overlooked the street and I had just been served a piece of pizza and a second cup of coffee when I saw Eligio Villagrán, far away but coming toward me slowly.

I wasn't at all excited about the possibility of talking to anyone, but it didn't look like I could avoid it. Without hiding anything I concentrated on the tasteless pizza that I was unenthusiastically working away at; at the same time I considered what navigators call a "collision course": a trajectory that inevitably leads to an accident, as when a ship heads in a direction that puts it fatally in the path of another ship. In this case I was the fixed point and Eligio Villagrán was the threat heading toward me.

Sometimes they would say that he couldn't keep his mouth shut for a single second. He talked compulsively, he never listened, he carried on a frenetic monologue, entertaining himself or in some way finding an equilibrium within himself. He worked as a film extra in the Churubusco studios; he specialized in cowboy movies since he had a Northern look, like someone from a cattle town or from Texas. He never took off the pointed boots or the leather vest with studs that he had kept after some movie or another. Adolescent acne, or maybe a flash fire from a gas stove, had scarred his face; it was a face that, for the price of a single ticket, offered a certain air of the Good, the Bad, and the Ugly at the same time, like spaghetti westerns.

I hadn't yet finished going through my mental card catalogue looking for all the cards relating to him when there he was, sitting in front of me, perfectly comfortable, leaning back in one of the chairs and smiling at me.

"Would you like a cup of coffee?" I asked him.

"You bet, partner. Let's throw back a few."

"So, what's new?"

"What's new with what?"

"Are you still in the movies?"

"Not much. You know that movies are dead. One with ponies, a commercial here and there, that's it. Getting by . . . Near Tula, some mountains, like hills of soft earth.

You ought to see how well it turned out. I mean, I think so. Damned dust in all directions. We ended up totally filthy."

"And so what had you been doing with yourself? Before that."

"That's what I'm talking about."

"But before that . . ."

"This and that . . . I was up north for a while, before the movie, I mean. We were working in Mexicali, and for a while in the Imperial Valley . . . And in Tijuana."

"What were you living on?"

"Asparagus at first. There's always something, you know . . . "

The heavy black clouds that only a few minutes earlier had covered almost all the buildings now began to move away, leaving a not-very-bright hole over the northern part of the city. I couldn't see the mountains surrounding the valley, but I imagined them. While Eligio kept talking, I thought that he wasn't the only one who didn't know how to listen. I put an attentive look on my face—a look of perfectly fake interest, like a listener on autopilot—and took advantage of the opportunity to let my thoughts guiltlessly wander where they wished. I couldn't quite tie together what he was telling me, when, out of the blue, to keep the conversation going, I asked, "Tula?"

"What? Oh, yeah. That was later."

"Let's get out of here," I said. "I've always wanted to take that way out and come back through Pachuca."

And it was true. Except for maps, I really had no notion where the Mezquital valley was, nor Ixmiquilpan, and I had never seen the Tula caryatides. I had heard about the candelilla plant, but all I knew about it was the vague impression that it was something the Otomí Indians scraped to make rope, a kind of maguey cactus leaf, or something like that. I had also heard something about the enormous flower gardens irrigated with water from the city's sewers.

We got into the Volkswagen and headed out of the city on the Naucalpan road. Eligio asked me to stop for a minute to buy cigarettes. I stopped the car in front of a liquor store. Eligio came back in a few minutes with a bottle of rum wrapped in brown paper. We got back on the road to Querétaro. In the background, an indiscernable and shifting point of departure, the dark clouds receded ponderously in the opposite direction from the one we were taking, perhaps because of a high wind and not just because of the speed with which we were heading off into the afternoon that, because of a directional sign and a detour arrow, began to grow lighter. Eligio took a nip from the bottle as he told me that he had had to get out of Tijuana quick.

"It was an emergency, partner. Things started going down heavy, you know."

"So what's happening up there? Lots of Americans, right? So they say."

"People who lost it all. Lots of old folks on the coast, in bungalows, just like in Álamos."

We got off the superhighway shortly after that and took a narrow, winding road. Tula's church steeple appeared and disappeared depending on the curves and our vantage point. We passed a group of dark, sheet-metal sheds that looked like a foundry. Further on my touristy curiosity was not strong enough to ask Eligio or anyone else about those huge installations that looked like a cement factory. Laziness or lack of interest has often prevented me from asking directions for some street in an unknown city; I've always preferred to figure it out myself or to chance getting lost. Things always appear by themselves eventually. It was better to imagine them, enjoy them, recognize them in their possible ambiguity.

"What happened is that we went inside these half-built houses," Eligio was telling me, "and there we got into an argument with somebody."

I didn't continue the conversation because I didn't want to give him the impression that I was just going along with him, and also because soon we saw people along the sides of the street, women and children unhurriedly coming out of mass, and a little farther ahead various cars from the capital parked near the church.

Later, as we were walking among the houses, following the path heading up the hill through lead-colored earth and passing a kid selling a little fused sand figure of a caryatide, I supposed that surely those sheds at the entrance to town were a cement factory. There was dust everywhere. Everyone had dusty shoes and feet, dusty hair and faces. A very strong odor wafted by and suddenly dissipated, as if the town had drainage problems.

We climbed over the pass toward the caryatides. I had seen them on postcards. Various columns lined up on a promontory. And then elongated figures, much, much taller than I had imagined: the Atlantans.

"A half-built house?" I asked.

"There were two houses, on the outskirts of Tijuana. Abandoned. They had brick-colored tile roofs, a little cone shaped, a little rounded, like Chinese straw hats. They would have been very pretty if they had been finished. Unpainted, concrete walls. They said they belonged to some guys, who were very well known around there, who had been in the Tijuana prison, and that's why they were unfinished. They belonged to these brothers who worked in contraband. They called them Los Brothers."

"Couriers or Mafia?"

"All the above. They did it all. Very tough dudes."

"Listen, I hope we don't get caught in the rain . . . up ahead."

"After all . . ."

We got back in the Volkswagen after climbing down the soft earth hill and buying a fused sand ashtray with a Tula caryatide on it. A loudspeaker echoed below. Someone was dedicating songs to someone else over the radio. We slowly began to exit Tula, and behind us the words of a *corrido* ballad faded in the distance or sharpened with the curves:

> Traían las llantas del carro
> repletas de yerba mala
> eran Emilio Varela y Camelia la Texana.
>
> They stuffed their car tires
> full of marijuana
> Emilio Varela and Camelia the Texana.

We left Tula. We drove straight north. We never veered right and the sun kept setting. The terrain was flat in all directions, ample and terse, horizontal, like a dry lake bed. I used to believe that valleys were immense hollows, that there were narrow passages with isolated mesas in their depths, surrounded by mountains. Maybe it was because valley started with a *v*, or maybe because of how green my valley looked when you contemplated it from above. The thing is that here it was plains all around as far as you could see or until it clouded over, like a kind of circular pampa. Along the edges of the highway unpaved roads headed up toward the mountains. The sky turned black again.

I don't know if it was some association of ideas or colors, or if it was because of one of those things that occurs to you while driving down a highway, especially if the road is straight and boring, but it led me to think about the orientation system used by Japanese pilots during the war in the Pacific. It was based on the location of the numbers on a clock face. I told Eligio about it: "Straight ahead is twelve o'clock, to my left is nine o'clock, to the right is three o'clock. And behind us, obviously, is six o'clock. For example, here, at about two o'clock, we have to turn toward Pachuca, or toward Ixmiquilpan, I don't know. See? Here at eleven o'clock we have this cow."

Little by little we began to close in on the next town. I never figured out if it was Ixmiquilpan. I was waiting for some indication, no matter how small, that we were on the right track. I was just remembering that from there the sewage water went back to Mexico City converted into chiles, tomatoes, onions, lettuce . . . and so the cycle of life and waste generously closed in on itself.

There we were, in the middle of the street, lost, without knowing exactly in what part of the world we had landed, when a red-eyed old man came up to us, banged on the window, and stuck out his hand. I closed the window in a hurry and had to slow down the car because of the number of people who piled up around us. They stared at us sneeringly, making fun of us. The old man said something I didn't understand very well.

"What did he say?"

"Better not look at him."

"Listen, I don't think this is the Pachuca road. Which way do we go? Shit."

Some women left a church. Street vendors in the plaza packed up their stands or covered them with plastic. A bottle suddenly smashed against the back window. I reflexively accelerated, but only for a few meters. Part of the screaming crowd opened in front of us; we kept still, other campesinos turned back to the sidewalks. Then we saw a silver grey Valiant parked on one corner of the plaza. There was a man in a *guayabera* leaning against the driver's-side door eating peanuts. Inside, in the back-seat, we could see two other dudes in hats and a couple of rifle barrels sticking out of the windows. Dark blue letters spelling out the word POLICE crossed the doors from one side to another. One of the guys smiled. It was Sunday afternoon.

With the utmost calm and naturalness we finally asked about the road to Pachuca. A boy pointed back in the direction from which we had come and told us to turn around at the end of the plaza. I speeded up respectfully and turned around in two movements—not your typical three-point turn—just like the Texas patrol cars in the movies, and we went back down the road by which we had just entered the town. I felt we were doing all right; the road was heading east so we weren't going in the wrong direction.

We started to cross back through the center of town. A riderless horse let us by. As we moved forward I practiced defensive driving and stopped at all the intersections, taking advantage of the car's inertia to carry us forward. At the next intersection, exactly at nine o'clock and one block away, the silver Valiant with its dark blue lettering and the dudes inside suddenly appeared. Eligio acted like he didn't notice anything. Every once in a while he took a swallow from his bottle of rum. He wasn't talking. I stared straight ahead—at twelve o'clock on our imaginary Japanese compass—looking for the certain safe exit that was awaiting us at some distant point.

"Listen," he said to me. "Look."

"Yes. They're the same ones."

We saw them at every intersection, off to the side, on

every block. We kept on going in a straight line, yearning for the highway, and at each intersection, off to my left, exactly at nine o'clock, we saw the silver Valiant again. And the dark blue lettering.

Gradually and boldly we distanced ourselves from the town, heading toward the open road. The Valiant seemed to be escorting us, following us toward the outskirts on a parallel course through the well-marked streets of the town.

When we got on the Pachuca highway, silence. The only sound was the rumbling of the car caused by my stepping on the accelerator and felt as a vibration in my body.

"What were we talking about before?"

"Nothing, nothing."

I looked back in my rearview mirror. Nothing, no one at six o'clock I told myself, relieved. Despite the cracked glass I could make out the headlights of a truck that, far from closing in on us or trying to pass us, kept falling farther back behind our car. Eligio kept drinking, absorbed in thought. He passed me the bottle.

"Look," I told him. "There at about ten o'clock, in the plaza; it's Pachuca's clock."

I turned the headlights on. I turned on the windshield wipers only every now and again. The storm wasn't sure whether or not to hit us. The plaza was empty. We kept heading south without stopping. By that time of day there were hardly any cars on the highway.

"And the thing is we did more than just scare him."

"Who?"

"The dude."

"Oh."

It was over an hour later by the time we got back into the city via the Indios Verdes exit. Eligio was talking even less than before. It didn't occur to me to say anything to him.

"And the thing is we did more than just beat him up," he said a little before I dropped him off at a corner downtown.

I went back to my apartment with the caryatide in my hand. I put it on the table. I threw myself into an easy chair, unable to read, smoking, not doing anything. I went for a walk. I ordered an empanada and black coffee at the pizzeria on the other side of the street. "More than just beat him up," I thought.

I went back to my messy apartment with the dirty dishes in the kitchen; there were pieces of eggshell stuck on the wall, dried hard.

I couldn't sleep. I felt my heart beating in my eardrums. I turned over. Banging against the inside of my squeezed-shut eyes was the glassy stare of the old man in the Ixmi-quilpan plaza, the pair of houses with conical roofs in the Tijuana hills, the piece of rancid pizza. I kicked off one of the blankets. I turned to lie face down against the mat-tress. I stuck my head under the pillow and let my arm fall over the edge of the bed toward the rug. I felt my hand run into something: a small rawhide string, a shoe buckle, a woman's high heel. I grabbed the shoestrings, looked for the other shoe, rubbed the soles. As if it were the in-step of a foot, my hand pushed into where Laura's toes went, her foot, my fingers, her unpainted toenails, her stockingless feet. I wrapped my fingers in the shoestrings and tightened them as hard as I could, trembling in the darkness.

Insurgentes Big Sur

S o then you came here, to Mexico City, the DF, to
study law, to learn about the world, to take advantage of the city as a jumping-off place when you
wanted to visit Veracruz, the Yucatán, the southwest of
Tabasco and Chiapas. During Holy Week, Christmas,
May, or August you'd grab the Ado or Tres Estrellas bus
and head out for Michoacán or the beaches of Oaxaca.
That's why you came to the DF in 1960. To see Mexico.
To find out what the big deal was about this city that Pepe
Alvarado had talked about so much and with so much
love in *Siempre!*, to see how Efraín Huerta painted this
gigantic town in his poems, to discover just how New
York-like was the city of those characters from *Where the
Air is Clear*, Ixca Cienfuegos and Gladys García.

It was Mexico City—the heart, the central nervous system—the city that arrived in the movies they showed in
the Zaragoza theater back home: *Aventurera, Esquina Ba-
jan, Distinto Amanecer, Los Fernández de Peralvillo, Los
Olvidados*. You also used to imagine it from the sepia or

green ink engravings in magazines like *Box y Lucha* or from the issues of *Vea* and *Vodevil* that you consumed in drawn-out secret readings. More than one unequivocal sexual polarization of more than one Tijuanan adolescent would be determined by the naked women who posed in the sensational centerfolds of *Vea* and *Vodevil*. More than one image of femininity would define itself through the not-always false or insufficient pathways of representation and would shape itself in their midbrains—the peach's heart, an anatomist would say.

They were the women from the capital. There were also the rumba dancers: María Antonieta Pons, Meche Barba, Ninón Sevilla. But men would also turn up now and again: masked or unmasked men like the Santo and the Blue Demon, Alejandro Cruz peering out from beneath a sweeping cape (the face above the mask, as Sciascia would say) of the Black Shadow.

And you'd turn your gaze from one side to another, from Los Angeles to the DF and vice versa, like in a Ping-Pong game. You couldn't decide very easily which of the two poles most attracted you; it wasn't ever very clear to you if the innovations in speech and dress ("We just wanted to give a certain style to the streets of Los Angeles," Eddy Olmos would say later) came from Tepito or from the East Side.

And so you arrived (no one and a hundred thousand, Pirandello would say) in Mexico City in January 1960, and ten days later you had to go back to Tijuana because your father died. It was the first time in your life that you got on an airplane. It was a Aeronaves DC-9, white among white cotton clouds, with the desire to keep floating in space without gravity to shape them. You had never before experienced this dimension of fear, the fear of flying over a flat, incommensurable, deformed city, one that showed no discernable trace of any possible point of comparison with any of the most elementary Euclidian lines or forms of plane geometry.

You were not able to pull yourself out of the body into which you felt you were grafted. You had barely begun to recognize some of the streets and already you were on your way back . . . soon, you'd be on a Tres Estrellas bus: fifty-two hours of uninterrupted travel from First Street to Niño Perdido in Mexico City. The same feeling of flying out and then bumping on back diluted itself into the feeling that you had gotten stuck in some intermediate zone. Neither here nor there. After turning forty, with more than half of your life spent in Mexico City, you began to suspect that at some point in the road you had committed a mistake in sentimental navigation. You never made the city yours. You never felt that it belonged to you or you to it. A city, you thought, is like a person; you either understand it well or not at all. You can have a good relationship with London and not get along with Paris. You could insist on going back to Paris, just to fail again, or you could feel happy in Rome, in your element, as if you had spent your whole life there. You imagined—with that out-of-place nostalgia that consists of missing what you never had, with that intimate megalomania that loses all sense of proportion and doesn't know how to hide the parallels between one quoted name and another—the relation that Joyce must have had with Dublin, Stendhal with Milan, Capote with Manhattan, or Pasolini with Rome: a link, a complicity, an enduring love, a passion. And the fact is you couldn't feel that way about this city, you couldn't figure out where to grab onto it or where to wander through it late at night in the way that Borges "fatigaba" the streets of Buenos Aires or the gentleman Auguste Dupin wandered the paved sidewalks of Paris in the damp evenings.

Probably the city had no reason to have had the same medieval traces as Siena or San Gimignano, a shell-like spiral leading from the center to the periphery, a precisely human dimension. That was not its style, and it wasn't a European city, and it grew like crazy. Likewise there was no reason for it to duplicate the architectural stages of Barcelona: the Gothic core circumscribed by a walled pentagon, the nineteenth-century latticework with flattened corners at every crossroad. Nor should it have followed the model of New York's cross-hatching streets, nor the type of urban plan based on diagonals so typical of the nineteenth century, like the plan of Indianapolis that was transplanted to Tijuana in 1889. No, its chaos was always uniquely its own; it spread out with no plan to regulate its health or contain the speculation and real-estate corruption.

You, no one and a hundred thousand, arrived in Mexico City in 1960, and it took you three years to feel that you'd arrived, three years until you could finally sleep soundly in a bed that was in a room that was in an apartment that was in the Cuauhtémoc area that was in the city named Mexico. It took you even longer still to realize that you didn't live in Mexico City, that you didn't inhabit all of it, but that you only lived in a certain part of the city, in a particular zone, in a very delimited territory from which you had excluded, for two and three years at a time, the sight of the cathedral and the central plaza. You lived, maybe, in one of its suburbs, which extended from Insurgentes Sur to Viaducto Miguel Alemán, from there to Coyoacán and San Angel—the DF's garden area—a series of small, sunny, tree-lined towns within the large and alien city beyond.

Since you didn't usually think in topographical terms, your way of learning about the country tended to occur according to certain horizontal plans, as if you lived on a mesa with the same climate and the same atmospheric pressure at all altitudes. But all at once you woke up one day with the idea that the power—that public, federal, and centralized thing—was not only located in the middle, but also above. It was lifted to the top of the pyramid: the zero point, the nipple on the breast, the throne of power in the high valley. That's why, you thought, they always gaze from the top down. That's why power is exercised centrifugally, thunderously, implacably, arrogantly, pitilessly, from the top down.

The terrain is uneven, torn up. You don't live on top of a pool table or in the promiscuous byways that Hieronymus Bosch drew in the "Garden of Earthly Delights," among fishes and frogs, your tail spread out like a peacock's. Thus, despite the fact that you had spent half of your life on this mountaintop or high plain of Mexican power that takes advantage of the geographical segment located below and all along the Tropic of Cancer, the not-entirely-defined relation that had been going on in a trivial and dispassionate manner changed on September 18, 1985 and became something else.

You don't want to live in London or in Paris or in Barcelona. You want to live here because it's not so cold. Because your friends are here, and, as Henry Miller said, because here you have at least one important connection with some of the inhabitants. And suddenly it all fell apart. The city fell apart, like an exhausted and cancer-ridden mother.

The earth moved.

Mutilations created unification throughout the city, and sometimes you had the impression that in the DF it was very difficult to have a world (there are novelists with a world and novelists without a world). It was more likely that a provincial novelist would have one, although back home there was too much world and too little work, because in terms of the personal, you (no one and a hundred thousand) had gotten stuck between the provinces and the capital: you were not from the DF and not from Tijuana. You had been paralyzed in a literary no-man's-land where you couldn't figure out which was more false, the Tijuana aspect or the capital city aspect, and you never were able to understand very well the relationship between Henry Miller and the nocturnal desert of Insurgentes Sur even though you had some kind of association of ideas while reading *Big Sur and the Oranges of Hieronymus Bosch* while sitting in a Torremolinos bar. You had left a note for a potential story between the pages of the book for many years, and from a stool in Torremolinos you watched the Route 100 buses go by, hundreds of young people sitting at the windows and on the roofs on their way back from the national university, down the whole length of Insurgentes Avenue, guarded by patrol cars in a perfectly planned operation to remove them northward so as to prevent any breaking of windows or sacking. It was a secret fantasy, a few notes scribbled years ago between the pages of the book by Henry Miller, who had authored the desire. But it wasn't precisely a political fantasy but rather a choral fantasy, the paraphrase of an operatic motif.

If you would have had an observation point—so began the unfinished story—from the cabin of a helicopter, you would have been able to see how a large percentage of the crowd, sometimes shaping itself into a wormlike line or a chain of ants, was emerging from the university stadium and moving into the Pedregal de San Angel section of the city. At first the compact group of excited young people moved quickly in close formation, continually sharpening the point and knifing into the tall yellow doors that provided (or denied) access into the residential zone. But when they climbed the fences, the column of young people cracked open, and from high above they began to spill into the Pedregal streets as if a current of amphetamines were flowing through their blood.

Almost all the houses were hidden behind high walls. The Artigas estate accounted for twenty-nine square kilometers, and beyond its infinite gardens, a legally established right-of-way, it cut off the paved road toward the Desierto de los Leones section of the city. The golf courses were connected by tunnels cut below the public streets. The young people felt as if they had entered enemy territory when they discovered Lluvia Street, and they undertook an assault upon the stone mansions without any premeditation whatsoever, without any comprehensible strategy at that moment, and they advanced through the streets of the area down Niebla, Agua, Fumarola, Sendero, Cráter, Rocío, Huracán, Pirules, Nubes, Fuego, Picacho, Crestón, Llama, Meseta, Cantera, Pizarra, Piedra, Nieve, Vereda, Pradera, Valle, Lava, Risco, Cascada, Ciclón, Volcán, and Granizo . . . Cataratas and Alud.

Compositor: Impressions, A Division of Edwards Brothers, Inc.
Text: 11/14 Aster
Display: Template
Printer: Edwards Brothers, Inc.
Binder: Edwards Brothers, Inc.

2917